WITHDRAWN
UTSA LIBRARIES

INTRODUCTION TO MUSEUM EVALUATION

Minda Borun and Randi Korn, Editors

Roxana Adams, Series Editor

1999

Committee on Audience Research & Evaluation
of the American Association of Museums

PROFESSIONAL PRACTICE SERIES

INTRODUCTION TO MUSEUM EVALUATION

Copyright © 1999. American Association of Museums, Technical Information Service, 1575 Eye Street, N.W., Suite 400, Washington, DC 20005. All rights reserved. No part of this publication may be reproduced or transmitted in any form or media or stored by any means in any information storage retrieval system, without prior written permission of the American Association of Museums, 1575 Eye Street, N.W., Washington, DC 20005

The opinions in this book expressed by individual authors are their own, and are not to be taken as representing the views of any institution or organization, including the American Association of Museums.

Introduction to Museum Evaluation

Minda Borun and Randi Korn, Editors

Roxana Adams, Series Editor

ISBN 0-931201-47-0

TABLE OF CONTENTS

CHAPTER 4

Formative Evaluation: Does Your Exhibition Attract and Hold Visitors' Attention? Do Visitors Know How to Use Your Interactives? Do Visitors Understand Your Messages?

CHAPTER 5

Remedial Evaluation: How Do We Improve an Exhibition After Opening?

CHAPTER 6

Summative Evaluation:
Determining an Exhibit or Program's Effectiveness: What Works? What Doesn't? What Are You Doing Right?

CHAPTER 7

Issues in the Field

APPENDIX A

APPENDIX B

INTRODUCTION

A well-known and increasingly understood fact is that visitors' museum experiences are a product of both what the visitors bring with them, in terms of prior knowledge, leisure agenda, and social dynamics, and the ideas and experiences museums offer. Bridging the gap between visitors' expectations and needs and the museum's goals is the province of audience research and evaluation.

When institutions first begin thinking about their audiences and how to approach program and exhibit development from a more visitor-centered approach, they often begin by asking, "Who are our visitors?" Audience research can provide a wide range of information about visitors and non-visitors. Visitor demographics can be collected as a baseline against which changes in visitorship can be measured (e.g. as the result of new programming and outreach efforts). Having the most complete information about current visitors can also help institutions identify who their non-visitors are. Furthermore, audience research can support institutions' efforts to understand why various audience segments do not visit —what their perceptions of the institution are, what has prevented them from visiting in the past, and what experiences they value.

As institutions move from understanding who their audience is to searching for practical ways to incorporate the visitor perspective into programs and exhibitions, the focus turns to evaluation. Evaluation in all its phases (front-end, formative, remedial, and summative) provides remarkable information about visitors and how they experience museums.

Front-end evaluation examines content ideas during the initial planning stages of an exhibition or program to help planners understand how visitors comprehend and think about the proposed content.

Formative evaluation tests program components during the design stages to isolate problems in how visitors use and understand them.

Remedial and summative evaluation analyze visitors' experiences with individual components within the context of the exhibition or program as a whole. Remedial evaluation is conducted with the intent of making changes to the final product; whereas, summative evaluation is used to determine the overall effectiveness. Because of the valuable information evaluation and audience research can provide, it can be used as a means for museums' improving exhibitions and programs and as a decision-making tool.

This packet on evaluation is designed for full-time staff members of museums, historical societies, and similar cultural organizations who are not specifically trained to conduct evaluation or visitor studies. This collection of articles, including technical "how-to" papers and case studies, is intended for educators, administrators, project or exhibit managers, designers, and curators in any type of museum who design exhibits and programs and who are continually making programming decisions. The goals of this packet are to introduce the field of evaluation and audience research (including its terminology, methodology, and theoretical underpinnings) and to offer practical applications for all phases of evaluation.

Additional information about evaluation and research is available from the American Association of Museums Standing Professional Committee on Audience Research and Evaluation (CARE). CARE works to share the latest findings and techniques about audience research and evaluation, to bring high quality programs to the field through national and local forums, and to share and provide support and resources. The Committee achieves these goals first and foremost through active participation in the annual AAM conference programs and in the programs of the various regional associations. Such information dissemination efforts include sponsoring a poster session at the AAM annual meeting and publishing "Current Trends in Audience Research and Evaluation," a bound set of the presentations. Members stay further connected via the CARE newsletter. Beyond being an information source, CARE also guides practice through publication and maintenance of professional standards for the conduct of visitor research and evaluation activities.

CARE membership is open to all museum professionals interested in the visitor experience. Membership in the committee is separate from membership in AAM and is renewable each January. To join CARE, contact AAM.

Minda Borun, Director of Research and Evaluation,
The Franklin Institute Science Museum,
Philadelphia, PA.

Randi Korn, Director,
Randi Korn and Associates, Inc., Alexandria, VA.

CHAPTER 1

Introduction to Evaluation: How Can We Create Effective Exhibitions and Programs

CONVINCING THE DIRECTOR

Alan Friedman

Originally appeared in *Museum Visitor Studies in the 90's*, ed. by Sandra Bicknell and Graham Farmelo, London: Science Museum, 1993; also published in slightly different form in *Visitor Studies: Theory, Research, and Practice*, ed. by Don Thompson, Steven Bitgood, Arlene Benefield, Harris Shettel, and Ridgeley Williams, Jacksonville, AL: Visitor Studies Association, © 1993.

Unlike some other museum directors, I have become convinced that visitor studies, particularly formative evaluation, must juggle the competing priorities of my institution. Directors must juggle competing priorities, including collecting, conserving, publishing, maintaining exhibits, looking after the building, increasing visitor counts, and maybe even raising funds for a new wing. This paper is about how I came to hold the view that visitor studies are at least as important as any of these popular pastimes.

Directorial priorities are based on an institution's mission statement. My institution's mission is to communicate science and technology to children, teachers and families. Essentially all museums' missions include educating the public.

How can my board of trustees and I measure how successfully we communicate? By the square feet of exhibitions we produce each year? By visitor counts? Though easy to calculate, neither is a particularly meaningful measure of communication.

Formative evaluation is a type of visitor study, an iterative technique for measuring how effectively an exhibit prototype communicates and then revising it accordingly. Formative evaluation supports our mission, but it is not cheap and it does take time. It raises the cost and delays the completion date of exhibitions which are already expensive and time-consuming to create. Is it worth it? Formative evaluation is certainly not the cheapest way to build exhibitions, but I have become convinced that it is the cheapest way to build effective exhibitions. I have learned to give priority to projects which make use of this kind of evaluation even if the price must be paid by reducing the scale of the exhibition or cutting other costs. My conviction stems from 20 years of experience in developing exhibitions both with and without formative evaluation. I will give four real examples. In each case plans were drawn up by a team of experienced exhibition designers, scientists, and educators, drawing on shared skills, knowledge, experience, and intuition. In each case the team believed that the end results would effectively communicate science and technology to the public. Finally, in each case the director concerned decided whether or not to grant funds to the project and whether or not to divert some of those funds, perhaps up to 15 or 20 per cent of the overall project budget, to pay for formative evaluation. First of all I will describe the four examples and then I will discuss both the final decisions and the eventual results of those decisions. I invite you to consider what you would do in each case.

EXAMPLE ONE: ROULETTE TABLE

The study of chance—the statistics of random variations —is a fundamental part of modern mathematics and has had important applications in fields as diverse as physics, astronomy, environmental science, and traffic engineering. There is evidence that most people hold serious misconceptions about chance. Many believe, for example, that chance is history-dependent: if in a game of roulette odds win five times in a row, it is tempting to assume that evens are 'overdue' and that the next ball is unlikely to land on yet another odd number. Mathematicians assert that the chance of success remains equal for both odd and even numbers no matter how many times odds have won in the past.

As part of a large exhibition on mathematics at the Cité des Sciences et de l'Industrie, Paris, a novel exhibit was proposed to reveal and address these misconceptions. The plan involved building a real roulette table (complete with red velvet chairs) equipped with computers, keyboards, and overhead monitors. Each visitor selected his or her own betting strategy from a number of choices. For example, if a visitor believed that recent winners were 'used up' and unlikely to win again, the computer could be instructed to avoid those numbers. Conversely, if a visitor believed that recent winners were 'lucky', the computer could be instructed to bet on those numbers. The computer played several rounds of the game, betting for each visitor using the strategy selected, and showing the results. (The actual roulette wheel was not used.) The computer then quickly completed enough additional rounds to achieve a degree of statistical significance, and showed the total gains and losses for each player. The historical strategies gave approximately the same results as random guesswork with slight statistical variations. An explanation of the mathematical principles followed.

Would you approve construction of this rather expensive exhibit? Would you add significantly to the cost of the unit by approving formative evaluation before going ahead with the final installation?

EXAMPLE TWO: TELESCOPES AND AN ARTIFICIAL SKY

The Lawrence Hall of Science in Berkeley, California decided to create an exhibition on the tools of astronomy. Considerable misconceptions about telescopes persist. Most people believe bigger telescopes are able to make things look larger, but in fact magnification is largely independent of telescope size. Bigger telescopes have the one great advantage that they make faint things look brighter.

The exhibition plan involved real telescopes and an artificial night-sky window-mounted high above the exhibition floor. Visitors would be able to try large and small telescopes, vary magnification, change lens diameter, and use spectroscopes. A custom-built telescope was commissioned. To make it easy to use it had coarse and fine adjustments for positioning, a finder telescope for help with aiming, and a right-angle viewing eyepiece. The eyepiece allowed visitors to bend over and look down into the telescope at right angles to the axis of the barrel instead of being forced to crane back to look directly through the telescope at the night-sky "window" up above. The designers had one telescope constructed, and although it was undoubtedly expensive, they were pleased with the quality of the image produced and the flexibility of the controls. They were all set to produce nine more.

Would you approve the immediate purchase of nine more copies of the telescope? Would you ask for additional time and money to be spent testing the concept first through formative evaluation?

EXAMPLE THREE: TRANSFORMATION OF ENERGY MACHINE

As part of the energy theme in the children's area of the Cité des Sciences et de l'Industrie, one consultant suggested installing a reasonably inexpensive exhibit showing the transformation of energy from one form to another. The unit consisted of a hand-cranked electrical generator connected by switches to six devices which changed the electrical energy to other forms. A toy train produced motion, a door bell produced sound, a light bulb created light, an electromagnet generated magnetism, etc. Children threw switches to connect each device separately or in any combination. As more devices were connected and more energy consumed, the generator became harder to crank up, demonstrating the principle of the conservation of energy.

Bearing in mind that this exhibit would be relatively inexpensive, would you approve the building of the unit, and then move on to consider more difficult or expensive exhibits? Or would you pause long enough to say "yes" to investment in formative evaluation?

EXAMPLE FOUR: COMPUTER-BASED TUTORIAL ON HIV/AIDS

The New York Hall of Science had for some time used a computer-based exhibit to demonstrate something of the human immune system. Visitors went through sections on anatomy, invasion by germs, and the body's elaborate defense mechanism. Each section included spoken and written text, colourful cartoon graphics, animation, and sound effects. Evaluation indicated that the exhibit appealed to a wide range of visitors, and effectively communicated the ways in which the human body protects itself.

The exhibit team decided to develop a new unit expanding on the biology behind HIV infection and AIDS. One key goal was to address misconceptions about HIV, such as the notion that any form of birth control provides protection against infection during sexual activity. (Once the infection route of the virus is understood, it becomes apparent that only condoms or abstinence can provide that protection.)

The designers completed a unit in the same style as the earlier exhibit. Then questions were asked. Would the stylised, cartoon-like representation of the human body, used successfully in the earlier exhibit, remain adequate for this topic? Would more realistic drawings of human sex organs and intercourse prove necessary to alter widespread and potentially deadly misconceptions about HIV infection?

Would you allocate time and money to redesign the unit with visitors and perhaps develop a second unit for comparison?

THE RESULTS

In each of the four examples, the decision makers involved agreed to spend money on formative evaluation, although in some cases it was suspected by both the exhibition teams and the decision makers that little would be learned. In all four cases, however, major surprises were in store.

The roulette table proved very attractive, but highly ineffective visitors were disappointed to discover that the roulette wheel was not used, and that the results were given simply by the computer. Being able to watch the wheel spin and the ball drop would have been a bonus. More importantly, visitors were keen to discover who won, even if the winnings were small. Since statistical variations inevitably meant that one strategy won a little more (or lost a little less) than another, winners felt that their strategy had been vindicated. Few stayed to read the text on mathematical principles. This exhibit was deemed ineffective and unlikely to be improved significantly by minor alterations.

Nine out of ten visitors attempting to use the special telescope gave up after less than 20 seconds. The number of controls confused visitors. The right-angle viewing eyepiece meant that visitors were unsure where the telescope was pointing. Modifications were made and instructions put up, but these made little difference. Finally the exhibit team abandoned this design. A much cheaper, less flexible, less comfortable, but simpler design was selected. Nine out of ten visitors succeed in making this new telescope work within 20 seconds, and stayed on to complete the activity.

The transformation of energy machine was attractive and visitors reported learning from it—but not learning what the designers intended. When both the bell and the train were connected, for example, young visitors reported that they had discovered that the bell was a speedometer that rang louder when the train ran faster. When all the switches were thrown, the generator became hard to turn: visitors decided it was malfunctioning. The generator was seen simply as a device to turn the exhibit on; none of the visitors seemed to have learned anything about energy transformation. The designer reluctantly concluded that the exhibit tried to do too much and that the topic would be better explained by a series of generators connected permanently to one or more of the energy-consuming devices, a much more expensive but also a much more effective design.

The HIV/AIDS exhibit managed to communicate some of the basic biology of the virus, but most visitors went away still thinking that any form of contraception can prevent transmission of the disease. A more explicit depiction of intercourse was tested, and although it did not approach the realism of photography, this version made a big difference to understanding. Twice as many visitors left understanding the efficacy of condoms as opposed to other methods of birth control. For example, correct answers to one question on condoms versus diaphragms rose from 22 percent to 45 percent of visitors tested.

THE LIMITS OF INTELLIGENCE, EXPERIENCE AND INTUITION

Some exhibit designs surely do work well the first time. In the absence of visitor studies, however, we never know whether they work or not. As the examples above demonstrate, even talented, experienced exhibition teams may sometimes produce designs which prove to be ineffective, frustrating, or even counter productive in communicating with visitors.

Had the decision makers in each institution approved these exhibits as originally designed, the result would have produced value in terms of exhibits produced per dollar spent. The exhibits would nevertheless have given very poor value in terms of science and technology communicated per dollar spent. Formative evaluation allowed ineffective exhibits to be abandoned or transformed into effective exhibits.

Repeated experiences like these have convinced me that visitor studies are high-priority management tools. At the New York Hall of Science we use front-end and formative evaluation whenever possible for static and interactive exhibits, for demonstrations and for education programs.

SECONDARY BENEFITS

Evaluation also has important secondary benefits for directors. It keeps staff concentrating on how museums affect visitors rather than on the myriad of other priorities competing for their time. Evaluation encourages teamwork, because prototype construction and statistically significant visitor testing are difficult to perform solo. It helps visitors feel that they can have a hand in creating the museum, rather than simply passively viewing the work of remote scholars. In a science museum, evaluation keeps staff actively using scientific methodology and values, not just talking about them.

THE BOTTOM LINE

The most fundamental value of visitor studies lies in their relevance to mission statements. Balanced budgets, happy trustees, contented staff and proud funders are all highly desirable, but these do not tend to be reflected in mission statements. Changing visitors by helping them to question, to learn and to be curious—this is the kind of thing demanded by mission statements. Visitor studies allow us to maximize our impact on visitors, and also to know whether we are succeeding in what we set out to do.

Alan Friedman is director of the New York Hall of Science

STUDYING YOUR VISITORS: WHERE TO BEGIN

by Randi Korn

Reprinted by permission of the American Association for State and Local History, *History News 49* (March 1994): 23-26.

More and more museums are beginning the respectable yet arduous task of studying their visitors. While people have been visiting museums for years, it is only recently that museum practitioners have become interested in understanding their visitors' museum experiences.

Visitor evaluations can take many forms—there really is not a single perspective or approach that is considered the norm. There also are many circumstances under which visitors are studied: in exhibit settings; during school visits; in interactions between individual visitors and objects. Often the jargon, coupled with the variety of methodological options, are enough to turn people away. However, as visitor studies become more accepted and practiced, everyone working in museums and historical organizations will benefit from sharing a common understanding of the terminology and procedures used in these studies.

The purpose of this article is two-fold. First, it clarifies and defines evaluation terminology. As with any young field, new names and definitions often emerge, sometimes replacing ones that were once well understood. An up-to-date review of the current terminology is presented here. Second, this article also provides beginners with some general information about conducting simple visitor evaluations. At the least, this will give practitioners a feel for the range of visitors' experiences and an idea about how to begin thinking about evaluation.

VISITOR STUDIES

Thirty years ago when "evaluation" was the "E" word, there was only summative evaluation. Evaluation and summative evaluation were synonymous. If a museum evaluated a program, it conducted a summative evaluation. Evaluation, if done properly, can serve as a decision-making tool. It provides information about a program—from the user's perspective—that determines the program's successes and shortcomings and helps make decisions about the program's future. Evaluation data are always collected systematically and deliberately.

Summative evaluation is when evaluative information is collected at the end of a program or after the installation of an exhibit. When museums began evaluations, summative evaluation was the norm and exhibits were the only type of program that was studied. Evaluation findings that suggested changes be made to the exhibit were often ignored because of budgetary and logistical constraints. Thus, the idea of formative evaluation was adopted.

Formative evaluation tests program components during the design stages to isolate problems such as the placement of exhibit components or the content of a label. It is most often used during exhibit development. Formative evaluation is an iterative process. That is, once problems are realized, corrections are made and retested until the component achieves the desired results based upon stated goals and objectives. Interactive audio visual components, directions to interactives, labels, graphics, and headings can all be tested using inexpensive mock-ups. The practice of formative evaluation in museums became so instructive that exhibit developers soon realized that they might benefit from conducting evaluations earlier in the exhibit development process-during the exhibit's concept development stage.

Front-end evaluation tests concept ideas during the initial planning stages of an exhibit. Visitors' familiarity with and preconceptions of the subject matter are often examined as are their general understanding of exhibit themes.

As museum practitioners become more familiar with evaluation as a process, they are also becoming more comfortable with the idea of change. The words "process" and "change" are important. Since the visitor experience and the relationship between visitors and exhibits, for example, are not yet fully understood, museum practitioners should accept that they are engaged in a learning process when they develop and create an exhibit or program. The idea of changing an exhibit component that is not quite right, for example, is far more acceptable now than it was when exhibit evaluations were first conducted.

Evaluation procedures can be applied to all types of museum programs. However, exhibits are the program type used throughout this article to help explain and describe evaluation. Readers should acknowledge that the information contained here can be applied to all types of programs at museums and historical organizations.

GETTING STARTED: FRONT-END EVALUATION

Front-end evaluation helps planners understand how visitors comprehend and think about the ideas that will be displayed in the exhibit. It is conducted in search of the "hook" that will draw visitors into the subject matter. Front-end evaluators hope to find the common ground between visitors and the exhibit.

There are no hard-and-fast rules about what one should explore during a front-end evaluation. It depends on the goals and objectives of the exhibit—that is, what the team hopes visitors will experience, do, and/or understand. Front-end evaluation, however, only works if the planning team has a vested interest in developing an exhibit that is both audience-driven and institutionally-driven.

The museum experience is the product of interactions between visitors and the exhibit and the conceptual framework in which the objects are presented. Visitors are complicated. They have life experiences and knowledge that affect how they interact with and experience an exhibit. Mixing these two forces—visitors and the exhibit—creates the visitor experience. Front-end evaluation gives museum practitioners a chance to learn about museum visitors and the potential of the visitor experience in the context of their exhibit idea. The museum, however, must relinquish some of its power and share it with visitors, if visitors are to have significant and memorable experiences. (A good example of front-end formative evaluation may be found in the 1993 article "Evaluation Methods and Findings Shape Ideas for a Junior Gallery" by Randi Korn in Visitor Studies: *Theory Research and Practice*, vol. 5, Jacksonville, Alabama Center for Social Design.)

Since it is usually conducted before an exhibit is built, a context must be created for the front-end evaluation. Relevant objects in another exhibit hall of the museum, photographs of objects, or even books usually suffice for these preliminary procedures. Front-end evaluators usually ask the following questions:

What do visitors think about when confronted with specific objects and/or ideas?

What meaning emerges from their encounter?

Which objects catch visitors' attention? Why?

Are memories awakened as visitors look at objects? If so, what are they?

How much do visitors know about this subject matter or topic?

What do visitors imagine they will learn in the exhibit?

What do visitors imagine they will see in the exhibit?

What do visitors imagine they will experience in the exhibit?

Asking visitors knowledge-based questions is perhaps the most difficult aspect of a front-end evaluation. Sometimes visitors feel awkward and uncomfortable, especially if they are not knowledgeable about the subject matter. Knowledge-based questions, therefore, must be carefully designed. Some evaluators have successfully designed game-like activities for visitors that provide useful information while easing visitors' stress levels.

Typically, front-end evaluators conduct face-to-face interviews asking open-ended questions. Open-ended questions allow visitors to describe their experiences in their own words as opposed to having them fit their experiences into the predetermined, museum-generated responses that usually appear on standardized questionnaires. Standardized questionnaires are very useful for some kinds of visitor studies, but at these early stages of exhibit development, it is useful to ask-open ended questions to encourage visitors to think and speak freely about a topic. (A good resource for this is Ralphling and Serrell's "Capturing Affective Learning" found in Volume 7 of Current Trends in Audience Research and Evaluation published in 1993 by the AAM Committee on Audience Research and Evaluation.)

Before talking with visitors, choose a target sample. The target sample may be determined by the goals and objectives of the exhibit. For example, if the exhibit is designed with the adult visitor in mind, your sampling and recruitment strategy should target adults. Sample sizes for front-end interviews can range from 35 to several hundred depending on the methodology. Open-ended interviews usually require a smaller sample than standardized questionnaires.

Front-end evaluation results can gently remind exhibit developers of how nonexperts approach, think about, and understand an idea. In their article "Psychology and the Museum Visitor" (Manual of Curatorship: A Guide to Museum Practice, ed. John Thompson, London: Butterworths, 1984) Michael Alt and Stephen Griggs articulated this point very well when they said, "The answer lies not in the exhibit, but in the way the visitors perceive the exhibit. An understanding of how people respond to exhibits requires an understanding of people, not exhibits."

MOVING FORWARD: FORMATIVE EVALUATION

Formative evaluation is conducted during the design stages of an exhibit or program using inexpensive prototypes. Labels, interactives, gallery guides, and other exhibit components would benefit from formative evaluation. Formative evaluation detects and isolates problems early in the design process—before building the final product. The goals and objectives of the exhibit, individual components, and labels, however, must be clarified before beginning the evaluative process. They are necessary for determining the success of the components being tested.

Formative evaluation is less formal than some of the other evaluation methods in that often it is not necessary to generate written reports, since changes to the exhibit could happen very frequently. This does not mean, however, that formative evaluation is not thoughtful or systematic. Data collection for formative evaluation, like all evaluation types, must be systematic and unbiased. Formative evaluation can uncover quickly what is not working quite right in terms of accessibility, visitor comfort, and visitor comprehension. Formative evaluators ask relatively simple, uncomplicated questions such as:

Are the instructions clear?

Are visitors using the interactives as intended by designers?

Are visitors understanding the message as intended by exhibit developers?

Are the section headings strategically placed?

Can visitors see the cased objects? Is the interactive too long?

Are the labels legible?

Is the content of the labels and gallery guides clear?

What general meaning are visitors creating from their experiences?

Formative evaluation data can be collected by observing and/or interviewing visitors. Observations provide an objective account of visitors' experiences while interviews provide constructive feedback from the users of the exhibit. In interactive galleries, observations can suggest which components attract visitors and which do not by simply recording how many visitors approach the displays and how many bypass them. Informal visitor interviews can then inform planners as to the reasons behind visitors' behaviors. If visitors' remarks suggest that there is a design or installation problem (as opposed to visitors' personal preferences), changes can be made to the prototype to alleviate the problem. Changing a prototype does not automatically mean success will be met. The process of retesting and changing prototypes should be repeated until desired results have been achieved—again, using the goals and objectives as the measure of success.

Sometimes visitor interviews are conducted with cued visitors. This means that a visitor is recruited to view the exhibit knowing that he or she will be asked a few questions afterwards. The thinking behind this strategy is that visitors pay more attention to an exhibit if they know they will have to answer questions. If cued visitors do not understand the content of an exhibit, uncued visitors will definitely not understand it.

Label testing is usually done in the formative stages of an exhibit's development. Label writing continues to be one of the greatest challenges for museum practitioners. Label testing generally focuses on three issues: legibility, readability, and comprehension. Several researchers have tested different type sizes and styles to determine which are most legible. In addition, the Americans with Disabilities Act (ADA) provides useful recommendations. It is worthwhile to review the existing literature before making typographical decisions. Museum practitioners may want to reference either Elizabeth Ziebarth and Zahava Doering's Accessible Exhibitions: Testing the Reality (Smithsonian Institution, 1993) or Lisa F. Wolf and Jeffrey K Smith's "What Makes Museum Labels Legible?" (Curator, 36(2) 1993). Important considerations are that the type size be large enough for visitors to read, the type style be legible, and that there is sufficient contrast between the color of the letters and the background.

Visitors' comprehension of a label can be assessed by asking two questions. First, are there words and/or phrases that visitors do not understand? Second, are visitors able to paraphrase the label according to the stated communication objective of the label? As stated above, each component in the exhibit (including labels) should have a communication objective by which to measure visitors' remarks.

Since problems tend to rise to the surface quickly during formative evaluation, large sample sizes are not necessary. Sometimes planners are too close to the project to see the most obvious obstacles. Solutions, however, are often relatively easy to generate because the problems are usually isolated and very specific.

FINAL PRODUCT: SUMMATIVE EVALUATION

Front-end and formative procedures examine visitors' experiences with exhibit parts out of context. Summative evaluation examines visitors' experiences with individual components in a completed exhibit hall. It also examines visitors' experiences in the exhibit as a whole unit. Summative evaluation is also important because it invariably considers design factors (such as traffic flow and the placement of exhibit components) that appear only after the installation, but likely affect visitors' experiences.

Summative evaluation is the most formal of the three main types of evaluation. Larger sample sizes are sought and a variety of instruments are used to collect the range of visitors' experiences. Outside consultants are often contracted to conduct summative evaluations because objectivity is considered paramount.

The objective of a summative evaluation is to determine the overall effectiveness of the exhibit as well as the effectiveness of individual components. Visitors' behaviors and experiences in the exhibit are typically compared to the exhibit's goals and objectives stated at the onset of the project. The following are examples of questions a summative evaluator might ask:

What meaning (in the broadest sense) has the visitor created from his/her experience?

Which parts of the exhibit were confusing/understandable?

Which parts of the exhibit were most compelling?

Are visitors operating the interactives properly?

Do visitors see the brochure displayed in the gallery?

Which components attract the most/least attention?

Which components hold visitors' attention?

Did visitors read the labels? Which ones? For how long?

What did visitors do when they stopped at a component or exhibit case?

How much time do visitors spend in the exhibit hall?

What did the visitor learn?

Questions like these usually determine the evaluation instruments. For example, tracking visitors through an exhibit will determine which components attracted the most/least attention and how much time visitors spent at each component and in the hall. Tracking visitors means that visitors' behaviors are observed and recorded, usually onto a map representing the gallery space. A stopwatch is often used to time how long visitors stay at individual components, labels, and in the whole exhibit area. Tracking is a very labor-intensive procedure, but is worthwhile as it provides an objective account of visitors' behaviors.

Visitor interviews determine the meaning visitors created from the exhibit and which parts were understandable and/or confusing. Visitors' descriptions of their experience are compared to the exhibit's goals and objectives to determine the effectiveness of the visitor experience from the museum's perspective and quality of the visitor experience from the visitor's perspective. Visitors' experiences often include unexpected outcomes—ones for which the museum did not necessarily plan. These experiences are not less important, however. They suggest the complexity and diversity of the visitor experience and demonstrate how difficult it is to anticipate what happens when visitors interact with an exhibit. Front-end and formative evaluation minimizes, to a certain extent, some of the surprise results found in a summative evaluation.

The successes and shortcomings of public programs such as adult classes, docent tours, or special events programs are usually assessed by summative evaluation. Typically museums distribute short forms that ask visitors a series of questions about the quality of the program. These types of forms are widely used because they are easy to produce and administer. They usually focus on visitors' general satisfaction, but tend not to provide constructive criticism for program developers who wish to understand the details of the visitor experience. This is mostly due to the nature of the methodology (often respondents are self-selected, not randomly selected) and the inexperience of staff members who prepare the forms.

Other methodologies are available, but they are more time consuming and difficult to conduct in the context of a public program. Interviewing program attendees just after they have finished a tour, for example, would produce very useful information, but is logistically difficult (especially if there is only one interviewer). Some attendees, however, may be willing to be interviewed by phone at a later date and would, if asked, provide the museum with their name and phone number before leaving the museum. Collecting in-depth information from a sample of visitors who have attended a program can be quite useful to program planners.

Another useful strategy is observation. Observing and recording visitors' behaviors and comments/questions on a tour can indicate weak parts of the tour (when visitors' attention appears to be waning), the level and quality of interaction between tour guides and visitors, the content and quality of the questions being posed by guides and visitors (especially in tours for school- children), and the visitors' visible level of comfort and interest. Conducting such observations are labor intensive, but worthwhile because they document the interactive process. While it is advantageous to have a relatively objective and skilled observer conduct the observations, they can also be conducted by a trained educator as he or she likely has a strong sense of what comprises quality educational interactions and has conducted observations as part of a training process.

Evaluation studies can be very instructive planning tools. The goals and objectives of the evaluation, however, must be articulated as they typically guide the evaluation process from the first staff meeting through data analysis. Staff members must also be sure that they are asking the right questions in the right way. Questions should be asked only if they will provide useful information, and they should not lead the visitor to respond in a particular manner. Pre-testing all evaluation instruments will help detect design flaws. For example, if all visitors are answering one of the questions in the same exact way, the question may be biasing visitors to respond in that way.

Evaluation, if it is slowly integrated into the operations of a department, or even the museum, will serve staff members well. Understanding programs and exhibits from the visitors' perspectives will help museum practitioners improve the quality of their work. Evaluation results, if acknowledged and used, can support change and move the museum forward.

Evaluation specialist Randi Korn conducts evaluation and research for museums and cultural organizations nationwide.

CHAPTER 2

Visitor Surveys: Who Visits and Who Doesn't?

GETTING STARTED IN AUDIENCE RESEARCH

Marilyn G. Hood

Reprinted from *Museum News*, volume 64 (February 1986) 25-31.

You want to learn about your audiences—the people who visit your museum and those who do not—but you don't know where or how to begin.

That's a common dilemma for museum personnel, who recognize that getting some solid information about what people expect from a museum experience, how they react to exhibits and programs, and how they learn in museums can help improve staff decisions about programming, exhibit design, learning opportunities and audience development. But where do you start? What method will you use—visitor interviews, telephone survey, observation study? How do you develop a plan? What groups of people will you study—and how will you choose your sample? Who will carry out the project?

To assist your thinking on how to get started, this article lays out some of the options to be considered. There is no one method universally applicable to all museum audience research situations. The essential requirement is that whatever option you choose, for whatever size project, the study should be carried out with thoroughness and precision.

Since the ultimate goal of all research is to produce quality information for decisionmaking, the first step in any research project is to identify the issue you hope to resolve through the study. What puzzles you about how people do or don't respond to your exhibits and programs and to the museum in general? What information will help you do a better job, will aid your planning and making choices? Specifically, what does the museum need to know, from whom, under what circumstances, and for what purpose? If you do obtain these data, what difference will it make? How will both the museum and its audiences benefit?

Next, think through and discuss the whole process, from brainstorming what you want to know to how you plan to apply what you will find. The overall concept that emerges from thorough discussion determines both the research questions and the appropriate systematic method for carrying out the project. It's only after you specify what you need to find out that you are able to frame pertinent questions to provoke relevant answers that can be applied to deal with current or future problems.

Then, outline the entire project on paper before beginning any phase of it: the intent of the study, how it will be conducted, who will carry it out, how the data will be analyzed and used, and the time, people, outside expertise, and money required. Many museum audience research projects have foundered because the concept was never fully defined nor was the process adequately described at the outset. The more explicit you are in delineating study purposes and in outlining the project, the easier it will be later to analyze and interpret the data and to use the findings.

Implicit in your decision to undertake audience research are three assumptions: You expect to make changes; you are willing to accept what the data tell you, even when they alert you that things are different from what you think; and you have commitment to the study from everyone who will be affected by the findings.

The surest way to impede application of research results is to impose them on persons who have no stake in developing the project. If the findings are controversial, the suggested changes can threaten status, self-esteem, and power bases. Therefore, everyone who is expected to implement the results must have the opportunity to give input to the design of the study. Also, if the director or trustees don't believe in the project, you'll never be able to use the results, especially if they reveal something these people don't want to know. In sum, if you don't intend to change as the result of learning new facts, don't do a study; you'll be wasting your time, effort, people-power, and money.

DEVELOPING A PLAN

How do you develop a systematic plan for conducting audience research?

Know what you want to know. Audience research is not a casual fishing expedition. You need a point of view, a focus around which to organize your inquiry so that all of the study components form a cohesive whole. When you know how you want the majority of the results to relate to each other, you can more easily formulate the questions to be asked.

To avoid merely repeating what has already been done, be aware of findings from audience studies that have already been conducted by museums and related educational and cultural institutions, such as performing arts organizations. Then you can frame questions that go beyond stereotypical demographic and participation data. Since the purpose of research is to learn something new, don't ask the question if you already have the answer or if it is available from previous studies.

Resources on audience research include articles in the major museum journals as well as specialized publications such as Leisure Sciences and The Journal of Leisure Research.

Know why you want to know it. Enumerate your reasons for doing an audience research project. They could include:

- to provide quality information that you can depend on, even when the findings are different from what you expect. Data that are valid (accurate, genuine, true) and reliable (consistent over repeated studies) can be secured when every step of the research is carefully structured and monitored. This is crucial because data that are not valid and reliable will lead you astray.
- to identify audiences, to find out who your current and potential audiences are. You can't effectively target your educational, audience development, or fund-raising messages unless you know something about whom you're addressing.
- to investigate audience expectations and needs. Remember the first commandment of education— "start where the learner is." You want to ascertain what current and potential learners expect of a museum experience. What do they need in educational offerings, information, and services?
- to evaluate, to get feedback on specific exhibits, programs, publications. You gather data about audience reactions in order to present your content and point of view more effectively in subsequent offerings.
- to set priorities, improve short-term decision making and guide long-range planning on programs, publications, services, physical expansion, and development and membership campaigns. You can determine if there is adequate public support to warrant embarking on an expensive project or sufficient interest in a proposed program.
- to learn why people do and don't come to museums by assessing their leisure habits, interests, preferences, peer group participation, and their evaluation of your competition. You will discover which audiences to develop only when you know something about their reasons for participation and nonparticipation, and about how your museum is regarded in the community (positive? negative? neutral?).
- to enhance your ability to act instead of react in a changing environment. You can cut your risks and plan the most productive uses of your limited resources of people, time, space, money, and energy by gaining knowledge about your environment.

After having satisfied the basic requirements of knowing what you want to know and why you want to know it (and being willing to accept and apply the findings), the next step is to answer the following questions: Who can give you the answers you need? Who will carry out the project? How will you conduct the research? How will you select the respondents?

Who can give you the answers you need? List in rank order all the current and potential audiences that could furnish the museum with useful information. Though visitors are handy, studying them may not supply the data you require. Members, former members, the business sector, or persons in the community who are not paying attention to you may tell you more of what you need to know.

First study the group whose responses will have the most vital impact on your decisions; then use these data to help shape research on the second most important group. It is better to plan to do a series of small studies over a period of time than to attempt one massive project. Each audience will provide one segment of information as you build a database about your publics.

Who will carry out the project? Whether you handle the complete process in-house depends on how soon you need the answers and how ready you are to learn the process. The more time and effort you invest in learning to do it right, the more you can do for yourself. Books on evaluation, question development, and research methods offer guidance, or you can employ an audience research expert for individual phases or the entire project.

Staff and volunteers can usually manage all aspects of a modest study, such as querying several hundred persons in the museum, by mail or telephone. You can hire expertise as needed on particular phases—questionnaire design, selecting a sample of the audience, training interviewers, interviewing, analyzing the data, statistical treatment. For a comprehensive study of visitors or community or outside groups that entails complex questions or analysis, mailing and receipt of several hundred questionnaires or coordination of a community research project, you can engage an audience research expert, a market research firm that specializes in consumer behavior studies and is familiar with leisure and educational research, or a university professor of leisure science, sociology, education, psychology, or marketing. When you get help from a university, however, you may have to do the project on its schedule and within its educational objectives.

If your research process involves interviewers, they must be committed to attend training sessions, to practice, to carry out their assignments precisely as directed, and to avoid interjecting their personal feelings or comments during interviews. If you cannot afford to hire a market research company to do the interviewing, a consultant can train dedicated volunteers and staff members.

The essential element is the existence of a system that is followed exactly. Despite your staff's creativity, energy, patience, commitment, enthusiasm, and cooperation, the project may take longer and be more taxing than originally judged. Should that happen, do not decide to do only certain steps and omit others, because every shortcut will undermine your ability to achieve worthwhile, substantial results.

How will you conduct the research? Different audiences require different research techniques and different techniques use various ways to record the information that is gathered. Among the recording forms frequently employed are questionnaires, observation forms, tally sheets, pre- and post-tests, tapes, photographs, and film. For the beginning researcher, it is advantageous to choose a method whereby the information can be easily recorded, analyzed, and interpreted. Usually this means an approach that asks definitive questions, uses a paper record, and involves analysis of the data by computer.

QUESTIONNAIRES

For the museum that primarily wants to know how audiences perceive the museum environment and its educational, cultural, and recreational opportunities, a questionnaire to gather data on audience characteristics, preferences, and learning responses is easiest to handle.

Visitor reactions to exhibits, programs, services, and special events can be assessed through self-administered questionnaires or by interviewers asking the questions. A questionnaire for all visitors or specialized forms for individual audiences will supply different types of information, depending on your purpose. Specialized audiences include teachers, adults accompanying children's and youth groups, children in school groups or museum classes, visitors to special exhibitions, community groups (Audubon Society, senior citizens, genealogists), people attending lectures, films or classes, and purchasers/renters of your space, services, and wares (bookstore, gift shop, restaurant).

A mail questionnaire is often effective with committed people such as museum members, nonmembers on your special event mailing lists, or members of another organization with interests similar to the museum's purpose. A mail questionnaire, however, is useless for a general audience because the response rate will be so low that the project will be a waste of your effort, time, and money. Be sure to send the forms when most people are able to return them by your deadline—usually not in summer, if respondents are likely to be on vacation—and include return postage.

For museum staff who want to know specifically how much learning has been accomplished, pre- and post-tests of the visit can be administered. To determine what your target audiences learn during their visit, you should test a comparison group that either does not make the visit or does not participate in the tested learning experience. Depending on your purposes, you may have the same sample of visitors take both pre- and post-tests, or you may have two subgroups (matched on such factors as education level and knowledge prior to the visit) each take one of the tests. Since there is usually a rapid decline in what is remembered after any event, the post-test ideally should be scheduled two to four weeks following the visit, rather than as the participants leave the museum. The assistance of university education departments is recommended for designing productive pre- and post-test research.

When docents take programs to businesses, community groups, civic organizations, senior citizen centers or schools, they can ask audience members to answer relatively brief questionnaires. This procedure may tap into groups that never come to the museum, revealing insights into why they don't come.

Interviewing at a variety of places where people gather—shopping malls, fairs, festivals, performing arts events, school activities—offers an estimate of community response to the museum, although these data will not be as valid and reliable as those obtained from a phone survey.

A telephone survey is the most effective way to acquire data from a truly representative sampling of the community, including people who frequent the museum, those who come only occasionally or for special events, people who may have come in the past but don't find it appealing now and those who have never come. Comparison of the data from all the subgroups indicates where the museum can improve its ability to attract and serve people who are apprehensive or diffident about visiting. Survey phone calls can be made by a market research firm.

The most comprehensive community research is carried out by a consortium of organizations—all the museums in a city, or a museum collaborating with a zoo or performing arts group. In addition to basic leisure participation and demographic data that will be useful to all the organizations, each may ask several questions about its own site or program. These data can be critical in convincing civic leaders, media and potential members and supporters of the importance of the institutions and their contributions to the community and of the need for increased support for educational programming.

NON-QUESTIONNAIRE INTERVIEWING

Techniques that do not use printed questionnaires, such as less formal conversational interviews, focus groups or panel studies, should not be chosen because they appear to be easier to accomplish. To produce worthwhile information, they must be no less structured and rigorous in method. Since the information procured is usually less quantifiable, these techniques are primarily valuable as initial steps to discern emerging issues, to get answers in the respondents' own words and to determine that the museum is on the right track in new ventures. Because these techniques depend on the moderator-interviewer's proficiency in directing the inquiry and in interpreting the data, they usually require guidance from trained leaders. The findings from these interviews, collected on tape, are very useful in defining questions for subsequent, more formal, studies in the museum, by mail, or by phone.

Individual conversational interviews demand preparation and skill by the interviewer, who uses a structured outline of questions or topics in a seemingly unstructured manner. Because the process calls for flexibility in following up on respondents' comments as well as in covering the research questions, it is actually more difficult for the beginner to administer than a questionnaire. With very young or very old respondents, however, this technique is more appropriate than a questionnaire. It can be used in the museum, at community sites, and all docent programs.

In focus group interviews, small homogeneous groups of people offer their impressions, suggestions, preferences, and expectations in response to questions posed by a trained moderator. Since this technique probes the underlying "why" of a situation, rather than trying to find an answer to a particular problem, it is especially good for testing new ideas for services or programs and at describing problems rather than arriving at solutions. Focus groups work well with people who are verbal and are not intimidated or easily swayed by others' opinions. Since selection of participants is crucial to the success of the focus group interview, assistance from a market survey expert or marketing professor is recommended.

Panel studies collect data over a span of time from the same group of respondents. If you want to check changes in opinion, perception, or learning over time, interview a panel of respondents monthly for several months or quarterly for a year, using face-to-face or phone interviews, or mail questionnaires.

OTHER TECHNIQUES

If you are doing an observation study, prepare a list of exact visitor behaviors you intend to watch for; never just wander around in an unfocused way, looking for whatever you can unearth. Instead, establish the participant information that will meet your research purposes and have all observers look for the same factors: activities engaged in; types of participants, their actions, interactions, expressions; movement patterns; and time and space descriptors. Since these studies are usually done as unobtrusively as possible, the recording form should be mainly a checkoff format, with space for noting pertinent comments by those being observed.

Other paper methods include asking visitors to sign a guest book, with their phone numbers and zip codes, and tallying license plates in the parking lot. In addition to providing an overview of where visitors are from, guest book signers can be telephoned later to solicit opinions on their museum experience or to ascertain what they remember of the learning opportunity. The zip code and license plate tallies give membership developers a clue to areas to target for direct mail campaigns.

Time-lapse photography has been employed in very large installations, such as World's Fair science pavilions, to discover traffic patterns, calculate holding power of exhibits, and furnish objective data on group behavior over a long period of time. More modest still photography or videotape documentation can supplement the data gathered by interview or observation. Again, adopt a point of view before you shoot: What pictorial information will help you make better decisions on future exhibits, traffic layout and services?

How will you select the respondents? Unless your target audience (visitor count, membership list, etc.) is small, you ordinarily do not study the whole group; you select a sample of the total audience. The sample size is not as critical as whether the sample actually represents the population from which it is drawn.

Depending on the audience size, sampling 10 to 20 percent is a good rule of thumb. Generally, the larger the target audience, the smaller the percent you need; a 10-percent sample of 5,000 members is adequate. For a mail questionnaire or visitor survey, 300 to 400 responses provide a good working number.

Drawing a "random sample" does not mean respondents are singled out haphazardly. Rather, a random sample is a carefully selected group of people, chosen by deliberate plan. If you stop people anywhere in the museum or shopping mall or pick names out of the telephone book, you will invalidate all your other precautions that are aimed at arriving at valid and reliable data.

When you are interviewing or distributing questionnaires in the museum, you can draw a random sample this way: First estimate how many interviews you need to acquire in a day or week, based on your previous attendance for a similar period of the year. Then, station interviewers at designated locations, usually exits, where they count off visitors (every fifth or tenth, etc.) to meet your desired sample size. If there is a group exiting, set a policy on whether you'll take the person on the right side and so on. The important element is that you have a predetermined plan and that it is followed meticulously.

To secure representation of all types of museum visitors, be sure to sample at all times of the day and week, both when you do and don't have special events. Provide a comfortable place for respondents and interviewers to sit, undistracted by noise and bustle. When interviewing or observing in the museum, remember that summer audiences are more likely to be tourists and winter audiences to be local. Choose the group that will provide the requisite information for your needs, or interview one-quarter of your sample in each of the four seasons of the year to get comparison data.

When you are interviewing in community settings like shopping malls, use a similar count-off procedure as recommended for the in-museum interviews. If there is not a comfortable place to sit, the interview must be brief and on a limited topic.

For a mail questionnaire, when you are selecting respondents from a list (your own or another institution's membership or class roster, for example), determine the size sample you need and the proportion of the whole list that is necessary for the sample. Pick a number between 10 and 20, count down to that number on the list, and then take every fifth or tenth person, for example, to make the sample size you want. Allow cushion for non-response due to lack of interest or time, change of address, illness, or death. If the group numbers under 500, ask all of them to respond.

On a mail questionnaire, don't be satisfied with a 20- or 30-percent response rate. You must expect to send at least two mailings to your sample members and if the return rate is still not at least 66 percent, to mail a third to the nonresponders. If, before you start, you are not willing to commit the time and money to do two or three rounds, don't attempt it at all, because the first wave of returns rarely is representative of the target population.

For studying the community, the most appropriate technique is telephone interviewing. However, since proper selection of telephone respondents is complex, involving random-digit dialing, you will need outside expertise in drawing the sample. Never use the telephone book to pick respondents because it is obsolete and does not include unlisted numbers.

These are some of the options to consider before you take any steps toward designing a questionnaire, interview outline, or observation form. In the design stage there are additional options to appraise, including those on how the data will be analyzed. Even if you cannot afford statistical and computer analysis immediately, it is still wise to build that possibility into the format, to allow for comparison analyses when you complete another study. The value of this more extensive analysis is that you can get several additional layers of information from your data, through cross-tabulating two or more factors, analyzing the variance between audience segments on learning styles, interests, or preferences, and investigating various relationships between psychographic, participation, and demographic data. Probing the voluminous data that already exist in your study results means that you will receive full benefits for your efforts in undertaking the project.

The most important outcome of conducting your first study is not gaining valuable information for current decisions on a specific situation, but making a commitment to research as an essential part of the museum's ongoing program. By developing a strategy that embraces research as an integral ingredient, you will be able to refine your research techniques, accumulate information on a systematic basis about all aspects of the museum and enhance your acuity about problems, trends, and accomplishments.

Though the emphasis on following deliberate, meticulous procedures may seem excessive at times, recognize that not following procedures will likely produce erroneous information, which can lead to disastrous decisions and actions if you mistakenly trust the phony findings. The time, energy, people-power, and money you invest in doing it right, on both large and small projects, pay off in valid, reliable information you can depend on when making your decisions.

Marilyn G. Hood is a museum researcher and consultant specializing in audience development, systems analysis and market analysis. She has a doctorate in educational communications from Ohio State University. She lives in Columbus, Ohio.

SELECTED BIBLIOGRAPHY

SURVEY RESEARCH METHODS

Alreck, Pamela & Robert Settle: *The Survey Research Handbook.* Homewood, IL: Richard Irwin, 1985.

Dillman, Don: Mail and Telephone Surveys; *The Total Design Method.* N.Y.: Wiley, 1978.

Dyer, Jean: *Understanding and Evaluating Educational Research.* Reading, MA: Addison-Wesley Publishing Co., 1979. (good basic text; explains terms very well)

Fink, Arlene & Jaqueline Kosekoff: *How to Conduct Surveys, a Step-by-Step Guide.* Thousand Oaks, CA: Sage, 1985.

Johnson, Janet & Richard Joslyn: *Political Science Research Methods, 3rd ed.* Washington D.C.: CQ Press, 1994. (comprehensive basic text; easy to understand)

Kalton, Graham: *Introduction to Survey Sampling.* Thousand Oaks, CA: Sage, 1983.

Lavrakas, Paul: *Telephone Survey Methods: Sampling, Selection and Supervision, 2nd ed.* Thousand Oaks, CA: Sage, 1993.

Parten, Mildred: *Surveys, Polls and Samples: Practical Procedures.* N.Y.: Cooper Square, 1966.

Sudman, Seymour & Norman Bradburn: *Asking Questions; A Practical Guide to Questionnaire Design.* San Francisco: Jossey-Bass, 1982.

CLASSICS

Cameron, Duncan: "How Do We Know What Our Visitors Think?" *Museum News*, v. 45, March 1967.

Cameron, Duncan & David Abbey: "Museum Audience Research." *Museum News*, v. 40, October 1961.

Crandall, Rick: "Motivations For Leisure." *Journal of Leisure Research*, v. 12, first quarter 1980.

Hawes, Douglass: "Satisfactions Derived From Leisure-Time Pursuits: An Exploratory Nationwide Survey." *Journal of Leisure Research*, v. 10, fourth quarter 1978.

Hood, Marilyn G.: "Staying Away: Why People Choose Not to Visit Museums." *Museum News*, v. 61 #4, April 1983.

Melton, Arthur: "Visitor Behavior in Museums: Some Early Research in Environmental Design." *Human Factors*, v. 14, October 1972.

Melton, Arthur: "Some Behavior Characteristics of Museum Visitors." *Psychological Bulletin*, v. 30, November 1933.

Robinson, E.S.: *The Behavior of the Museum Visitor.* Washington, D.C.: AAM, 1928.

Robinson, E.S.: "Exit the Typical Visitor." *Journal of Adult Education*, v. 3, 1931.

SELECTED PUBLICATIONS BY M.G. HOOD, IN CHRONOLOGICAL ORDER OF PUBLICATION:

"Leisure Criteria of Family Participation and Nonparticipation in Museums." *Marriage & Family Review*, v. 13, #3/4, 1989. (Also published in: B. Butler & M. Sussman, eds.: Museum Visits and Activities for Family Life Enrichment. N.Y.: Haworth Press, 1989).

"Application of Sociological and Anthropological Concepts to Visitor Research." *Third Annual Visitor Studies Conference Proceedings*, 1990.

"Significant Issues in Museum Audience Research." *Fourth Annual Visitor Studies Conference Proceedings*, 1991.

"Personality Puzzles." *History News*, v. 48, #3, May/June 1993.

"The African-American Museum Visitor: Who Comes, Who Does Not Come, and Why? The Art Museum Visitor and Non-Visitor." *Visitor Behavior*, v. 8, #2, summer 1993.

"A View From 'Outside'; Research on Community Audiences." *Sixth Annual Visitor Studies Conference*, 1993, published in v. 7, #1, 1994, Selected Papers.

"Comfort and Caring: Two Essential Environmental Factors." *Environment and Behavior*, v. 25, #6, November 1993.

"Relationship of Childhood Leisure Preferences to Adult Museum Participation." *Eighth Annual Visitor Studies Conference*, 1995, published in v. 8 #1, 1996, Selected Papers.

"High Response Rates are Critical to Museum Audience Research." *Visitor Behavior*, v. 11, #2, summer 1996.

THE ROLE OF THE INTERVIEWER IN SURVEY RESEARCH

By Zahava Doering

Reprinted with permission of the author. Doering, Zahava. Manual for Interviewers. In *Role of the Interviewer in Survey Research*, January, 1999, 5-17.

Conducting a survey requires a large amount of work on the part of many people, and an interviewer must be aware of the numerous processes involved in conducting survey research.

The diagram to the right is a simplified illustration of the steps involved in a survey. Start at the top and work your way to the bottom.

The interviewer is a vital link in the survey. Information depends on the skill and accuracy of the interviewer.

The interviewer's job is to collect the data from the respondents who, after analysis, will provide the client with required information.

Interviewing is similar to normal conversation but is more structured and specialized. It requires many of the social skills we use everyday such as courtesy, tact, polite assertiveness, and concentrated listening.

As an interviewer, you must establish a good rapport with respondents, maintain a neutral attitude, and convey respect for the confidence the respondent has placed in you.

Your respondent must be aware that all the information collected will be treated as entirely *anonymous.*

You must never divulge your respondents' names, should you know them, or any information given by them. We will never report individual data; all reports will protect the anonymity we promise the respondents.

THE WORK OF INTERVIEWERS

Data collection takes many forms ranging from short factual interviews to in-depth interviews about behavior, attitudes, and opinions. Most surveys use a *structured questionnaire*, i.e., one on which the questions to be asked are strictly ordered and most of the likely replies

STEPS IN A STUDY

1 Origins of a study: A "client" has a need for information which requires systematic data collection.

2 Developing the study

A. Develop the study design; overall approach and sample design.
B. Draft the data collection form: questionnaire, tracking form, protocol, etc.
C. Pretest the data collection form and methods to see if they work.

3 Data collection

A. Select or identify the population for the study.
B. Collect the data: interview, observe, track.

4 Analysis

A. Review & code data.
B. Process & tabulate data.
C. Analyze data. Consider implications.

5 Report results: "client" receives the needed information!

are printed. This article deals primarily with personal, face-to-face interviewing which uses a structured questionnaire. This article DOES NOT deal with in-depth interview studies.

SAMPLING RESPONDENTS

To speak to every person in the population would be impossible; therefore, sampling methods are used in surveys to allow us to select a random group to represent the entire population or a special group.

Information about sampling is presented later in this article. When interviews are conducted in a museum/zoo setting, we place *complete* reliance on interviewers since they will ultimately identify the people who are "in the sample" and must be interviewed. You must remember that the purpose of survey research is to maintain a profile of the population and NOT to describe the particular people who happen to be part of the sample.

WHAT HAPPENS TO SURVEY RESULTS?

Museum/zoo personnel use analysis based on data collected from visitors in many ways: to plan future programs and exhibitions, to assess current programs and exhibitions, to make changes, etc. Also, the findings of many studies can be of use to others. Visitor studies resources are continually being refined and expanded. Copies of studies are available to interested interviewers.

B. BEFORE INTERVIEWING

BRIEFING AND TRAINING

All interviewers working on each survey must be trained.

> In training, interviewers become familiar with the purpose of the study, the sample selection method, administrative matters, specifications on the particular study design, question-by-question specifications, and interviewing techniques.

The briefing provides a chance for you to raise questions and talk about any difficulties you foresee. Every question you ask will help other interviewers, so we welcome your active participation.

MATERIALS

Check to ensure that you have all the necessary supplies (provided by ISO) before you begin interviewing. You generally need your official name badge, a clipboard, sufficient questionnaires for the session, the survey fact sheet, a supply of respondent gifts, and several sharpened pencils. In addition, a mechanical counter and sample selection forms are important for the selection procedure.

For observational (tracking) studies, additional materials such as watches are needed. At the training session the method for storing and picking up materials will be discussed. It is the interviewers' responsibility to keep track of supplies and request materials, such as additional interviewer forms, when needed.

APPEARANCE AND REPORTING

An interviewer's appearance can affect the way in which respondents answer questions. If you dress in a "neutral" way, the chances of bias will be reduced.

A "neutral" style of dress varies depending upon where you are interviewing, but in general you will want to wear clothing that would be appropriate for the professional staff of the museum in which you are working.

On the other hand, for a tracking study, trackers should be as inconspicuous as possible and should dress more casually to look like a visitor or student. Tracking visitors is a form of *unobtrusive* observation. Visitors may alter their behavior if they suspect that you are watching them. Visitors should be unaware that you are observing them. In order to remain unobtrusive, trackers need to blend in with the crowd. You should dress comfortably in casual clothes. Do not wear anything or exhibit behavior that would bring attention to you. You should not wear clothing that would identify you as a staff member or volunteer.

Report early enough to gather materials and prepare so you can be ready to begin on time. Let your supervisor know *as early as possible* if you are not available to work on the days and times assigned so that you can be replaced.

C. CONDUCTING THE INTERVIEW

GENERAL GUIDELINES

One of the arts of interviewing is to put the respondent at ease and create a friendly atmosphere. **The critical moment is when you introduce yourself.**

> Interviewers who achieve the best results convey a study's importance by their own enthusiasm. It can be fun to listen to other people and learn about their opinions.

It is also important that interviewers never present themselves as "experts" on the subject matter of the interview. The less you know about an exhibition or subject matter the better; that way you can easily answer "I don't know" if the visitor asks if their answers were "right." Each respondent is an expert in his or her own opinions!

INTRODUCING YOURSELF

The simplest and quickest way to gain your respondents cooperation is to smile and greet him/her cheerfully.

Hello! We are doing a study of this museum, and would like to ask you some questions.

or

Hi! My name is ____ and I work for this museum. Today I'm talking to visitors.

> After a few interviews, interviewers generally develop a personal introduction with which they are comfortable. The key is to make the introduction quick and to the point.

EXPLAINING THE SURVEY

Once you have made initial contact with the respondent you may need to quickly tell him/her few things about the survey. In general, you want to begin with the first question as soon as possible. If there is some hesitation on the part of the respondent, you might say approximately *how long* the interview will take and mention that the survey is *voluntary* and that the results are *anonymous.*

Talk briefly and conversationally and, above all, be natural. You may need to vary your explanatory wording to suit the people you meet.

INTERVIEWING CHILDREN

Sometimes we wish to sample children's opinions in our study. In this case it is important to have a parent's consent before proceeding. This can be done casually: First approach and introduce yourself to the child and then, before asking the first question, ask the parent, "Is it all right if I talk to her/him?"

Usually parents are more than happy to allow their child to take part in the survey. Sometimes parents may seem reluctant or may want to answer the survey themselves. You simply state that you are particularly interested in children's opinions for this study, to hear their perspective would be a great help, and the parent is perfectly welcome to stay and listen if he/she wants. If the child is reluctant, you may want to mention that you have a postcard/ poster/gift as a thank you when the interview is completed.

ORGANIZING THE INTERVIEW

> When possible, lead the respondent to a quiet area, away from the flow of other visitors, to conduct the interview.

If the respondent appears tired, you may want to offer to conduct the interview at a nearby bench.

Ideally, the interview should be conducted without a third person looking over the respondent's shoulder. However, a large proportion of our visitors come in groups of two or more, and they are likely to be interested.

> Remember, only the respondent's views are required, and you should deal politely with third persons.

If a third person answers the questions for the respondent you should politely tell them that you are only able to record the respondent's answers. You can explain your choice of respondent by pointing out the corner and stating that you were assigned a certain person to interview as part of a random procedure.

In some special cases, third person assistance may be helpful. For example, in the case of a foreign visitor, a third person may be extremely helpful as an interpreter. An adult is often needed or required if children are being interviewed.

You must remember to face the respondent. If he/she is next to you, the respondent may read the questionnaire instead of listening to you. Familiarity with the questionnaire will enable you to concentrate on facing your respondent and listening well.

Respondents who have a physical or mental disability or who do not speak English are as much a part of the sample as anyone else. They should be given the chance to take part since their absence from the sample will bias the results.

Respondents may have questions about why the study is being conducted. Fact sheets, with contact information, are available for respondents to answer questions about the survey. You should never attempt to explain the survey's purpose to a respondent, even if the interview has been completed. Never allow a respondent to keep a copy of the questionnaire.

Avoid telling the respondent about your own background. Even an answer to a simple question about your work at the Smithsonian (for example) can influence the respondent's answers as well as elongate the interview. Gently return the conversation back to the interview questions and the respondent's opinions.

Other visitors will recognize that you are museum "staff" and may try to interrupt you while you are conducting an interview or counting. In all cases direct them to the information desk or the nearest security guard.

> In some rare cases a respondent may make the interviewer feel quite uncomfortable by their behavior. In this instance an interviewer should terminate the interview.

INCREASING THE RESPONSE RATE

"Response rate" means the proportion of people successfully interviewed out of the total number of attempts made. The response rate is a critical feature of sample survey work because a low response rate can cause bias in the results. The views of the people who are missed may well have been different from those who cooperated; therefore, the results of the survey may not reflect accurately the views of the population as a whole.

> Generally speaking, interviewers are able to successfully complete 8 or 9 out of every 10 interviews they attempt. In many cases, you can turn a refusal into an interview and improve your response rate by your manner.

The main reason given for refusing is lack of time. The important point is to find out the reason for the refusal so that you can persuade the person to take part; however, do not be too pushy. You will have to adapt your persuasive tactics according to the type of refusal. Some useful points to stress are the following.

> **Lack of time:** You can move quickly through the interview in FIVE minutes

> To people who say they have been **over-interviewed:** You are not conducting a marketing survey, and the results will be used to plan for the future with a museum/zoo visitor in mind.

> **To foreigners:** We are very interested in what they have to say, and you can speak slowly. If they are accompanied by someone, then perhaps the other person can help.

If, however, the respondent has made it emphatically clear that they do not want to speak with you, then do not attempt to convince them otherwise.

D. QUESTIONNAIRES

The main types of questions that you will encounter on survey questionnaires are **pre-coded** questions, **open-ended** questions, and **filtered** questions.

PRE-CODED QUESTIONS

Questions are "pre-coded" to save interviewing and data processing time. The interviewer circles or marks the appropriate coded response. A pre-coded question is preceded by a small oval or box for each possible answer. Remember that the pre-codes should NEVER be used as prompts unless the instruction "Read Out Loud" is given beside the question or you are using a response card to aid the respondent.

Did you find the exhibition... [Read out loud]

❑ Very crowded,

❑ Crowded, or

❑ Not crowded?

The pre-coded question form used most frequently in museums is one in which the codes are NOT read out loud. The interviewer classifies the answer into an existing category immediately OR records it for subsequent classification. Questions that have two or three logical answers are usually in this form.

Before today, have you visited other Smithsonian museums?

❑ Yes ❑ No

In many instances, more concentration is required on the interviewer's part in order to code the answer. Consider the following:

Who are you here with today?

❑ Alone	❑ Child(ren)
❑ One other adult	❑ Group of teens
❑ Several adults	❑ Tour group
❑ Adult & Child (ren)	❑ School trip
❑ Adult(s) & Child(ren)	❑ Other______

From the respondent's perspective, this is a question which he/she can answer in any fashion; however, it has been pre-coded into the categories of interest. Most respondents, in fact, name one of these. An alert interviewer can easily code the following answers to this question:

"My daughters." Or "My friend Joan and her two children." Or "The Senior Citizens Club of Helena."

For some questions, only the replies expected most frequently are listed and a space is left for recording OTHER:______

Answers that do not fit any of the printed pre-codes must never be forced into pre-codes. If an "other (specify)" category is not provided, and the respondent gives an answer which does not fit, write it down!

When in doubt about any response, write the response down on the questionnaire and it will be resolved later.

In the examples given so far, only one answer is possible. Questions that allow two or more answers are called "multiple response questions".

For which occasions would you consider a Smithsonian membership an appropriate gift?

❑ Birthday	❑ Father's Day
❑ Graduation	❑ New Home
❑ Wedding	❑ New Job
❑ Anniversary	❑ Other
❑ Mother's Day	

OPEN-ENDED QUESTIONS

An open-ended question is followed by a space on the questionnaire on which to record the respondent's answer in full, e.g.:

If you were the director of this museum, what one thing would you change?

____

____

____

Write down the respondent's answer word for word and make sure that the respondent has completed his/her response to the question. PROBE if necessary. By PROBE, we mean use neutral questions to encourage respondents to further clarify their opinions, provide additional information, or express additional ideas. Probing techniques are discussed more fully later in this article.

FILTERED (OR SKIPPED) QUESTIONS

Filtered questions are those which are not asked of all respondents. For example, a question about when the respondent last visited the museum would not be asked of a person who just told you this was his/her first visit.

Filtered questions are always followed by skip instructions:

Q1. Is today your first visit to this American History Museum?

❑ No

❑ Yes (go to Q3)

Q2. How many times have you been here before today?

If a respondent said "no", you would ask the next question, i.e. Q2. If a respondent said "yes", you would skip Q2 and ask Q3. You must always follow skip/go to other instructions carefully.

E. ASKING QUESTIONS

People who are interviewing for the first time often have concerns that they are "imposing" upon visitors. Often interviewers may approach timidly, not wanting to disturb the visitor. This often results in a refusal. Similarly, an interviewer may try to rush through an interview, trying to allow visitors to return quickly to their museum visit. It is important to give visitors enough time to answer questions. Even if a visitor begins an interview in haste, he or she will often "get into" the interview and give increasingly long answers.

PACE

Adjust the pace of the interview to suit your respondent. Remember that your respondent is hearing the questions for the first time. Most interviewers need to speak more slowly than they do in ordinary conversation. Be aware of how the interview is going and adjust pace if necessary. If the respondent is looking at his/ her watch you may want to reassure him/her with "just a couple more questions" or "We're finishing up now".

- The two most important things to keep in mind about interview pace:
- Read the questions aloud clearly
- Always give the respondent time to consider his/ her answer.

Look at the respondent as often as you can, especially immediately after asking a question. In this way, you are alert to signs of bewilderment or embarrassment. Sometimes you may need to repeat a question.

Make sure to keep the interview on track. If the respondent digresses into other areas of conversation, gently but firmly bring the focus back to the interview and continue with the next question. Try to interview at eye level when possible. If the respondent is sitting down, you should sit down as well. For an interview with a child, you may want to crouch down to his/her level, if comfortable. If someone is in a wheelchair, sitting on a nearby bench may be useful; otherwise standing during an interview is acceptable. In all cases, judge each interview situation independently and assess what you think would work best.

QUESTION ORDER

Ask all the questions in the order printed on the questionnaire. Ask every question, even if you think the answer has already been given.

Sometimes when answering a question, a respondent will also give an answer to a question that is asked later. Even so, ask the later question when you come to it. You can always introduce a question by saying, "I think you may have mentioned this, but…"

QUESTION WORDING

> Always use the exact words printed on the questionnaire. Ask all questions in a straightforward, neutral manner.

If you change the wording of questions, even in an apparently trivial way, you will introduce bias. Sometimes it is necessary in the case of foreign visitors to change questions slightly, if they do not understand the question the first time around.

If you ask every question in the same straightforward way, you are likely to get a straightforward reply. A note of surprise or disbelief in your tone of voice may cause your respondent to give answers which he/she thinks will please you or which the respondent thinks are "socially acceptable". Never apologize for asking what you may think are "difficult" questions.

GETTING RESPONSES TO PRE-CODED QUESTIONS

In asking pre-coded questions, you should try to get an answer which will fit one or more of the pre-coded answers without prompting. Several methods of probing are particularly useful, including the following:

Dealing with "don't knows"

Suppose that you ask a respondent—*On a scale of 1 to 4, where 1 means "not useful" and 4 means "very useful", how would you rate computer or interactive displays?*

You may get as answer such as—Oh, I don't know. I'm really not sure.

In such cases, probe with—Which is closest to how you feel? And repeat the question and the codes.

Dealing with vague replies

I answering the same question, a respondent might say—Oh, I suppose I find that relatively useful

In such cases, ask *What number on the scale would you assign to that?* And repeat the codes.

If you still get an answer which does not fit one of the pre-codes, e.g., *I'd say they are somewhat useful really*...ask them if their response means the same as one of the pre-codes.

None of these "probes" suggests an answer. They are used to guide the respondent towards giving a definite answer which will fit a pre-code.

PROBING TECHNIQUES

Probing encourages the respondent to express his/her own views on a question. If he/she needs help to do this, you can use a variety of probes

"Would you like to add anything more?"

"Could you tell me a little more about that?"

"Anything else you'd like to add to that?"

A questioning expression and a few seconds of silence until the respondent thinks of another idea often produce a good response. Sometimes the respondent will use vague words such as "good" or "interesting." Clarify the meaning by probing. For example:

"Exactly why do you think that is important?"

"What do you mean by interesting?"

"What about this did you find interesting?"

Another good method of probing is listening carefully to a respondent's choice of words, and then repeating words back to get the respondent to elaborate further. For example:

"You use the word 'haunting,' what do you mean by that?"

"When you say 'confusing,' what do you mean?

F. RECORDING THE ANSWERS

All information must be recorded ACCURATELY and LEGIBLY.

Use a pencil. Pencils are efficient and erasable and sharpeners are easy to include with the study materials. If you have to change an answer on a survey form, cleanly erase it or put two lines through the wrongly marked code.

Recording pre-coded questions. Fill in the appropriate circle. Sometimes you will write down an answer under "other (specify)" which you then realize fits one of the pre-codes. When this happens, cross out the response on the "other" line with two hash marks and initial it. Mark the appropriate pre-code.

Recording open-ended questions. Answers to open-ended questions must always be written out fully in the *respondent's* own words. In this way, the researcher receives the material directly and not paraphrased/interpreted by the interviewer.

G. CONCLUDING THE INTERVIEW

Always thank the respondent. Let the respondent feel that the interview has really been worthwhile and that you have enjoyed the interview. Leave every respondent feeling that he/she has made a contribution to the future of the Smithsonian, and would be happy and willing to cooperate again. Give them the gift.

Never leave a questionnaire with a respondent. If a respondent has additional questions, give the respondent the Study Fact Sheet and suggest that he/she write to the address on the Study Fact Sheet for further information.

Check your work. Glance through the questionnaire before you leave each respondent, or immediately after the interview, to ensure that every question has been answered. Check that:

A legible response is recorded for every question or in the space marked "Other____." If no response is recorded, the editors will assume that the question was not asked.

Odd circumstances or observations affecting the interview or any unusual answers are noted and explained.

Administrative items are entered. Do not forget to mark the status box, the location box, segment, and session.

Erase any stray marks. These will by picked up by the scanner.

Make sure circles are filled in properly (filled-in circles, NOT check marks). Make sure that marks do not go outside the appropriate circle.

Don't forget to write your initials or interviewer code at the top.

Unless the question specifically calls for more than one answer, only mark down the respondent's first answer.

For ALL refusals, please write down the reason on the second page AND:

DON'T FORGET to answer the questions marked with an asterisk (*). Information needed in most surveys includes residence ("Where do you live?"), Social composition ("Who are you here with?"), Age, Racial/ Ethnic identification, and Gender.

Zahava Doering is the director of the Institutional Studies Office, Smithsonian Institution.

WORKING WITH YOUR DATA

CODING AND HOW TO DO IT

by Randi Korn

Reprinted from *Visitor Surveys: A User's Manual*, American Association of Museums, 1990, 50-55.

Coding is the process of converting responses called data into numbers for later counting, tabulating or analyzing. In visitor survey lingo, to code means to assign one number to each possible response. Coding is directly related to data entry and to some extent, these two steps are considered together.

Although the coding process is not actually done until after the data have been collected, plan for coding now. Thinking through this step may reveal question formats that can be improved, inquiries that are not being thoroughly answered by the data, and more effective ways of administering the questionnaire.

Coding needs to be done whether you enter and analyze your data on the computer or run manual tallies and tabulations. Our examples illustrate a computer set-up for data entry using spreadsheets, which is compatible with many statistical packages. If your study involves more than 100 or so respondents and more than 10 questions, we recommend using the computer. The next chapter, Analyzing the Data, considers handy ways to maintain manual tallies for smaller studies.

Beginning on page 37, you will find the tables: Sample Newsletter Questionnaire, Table 4A; Coded Master Sheet for Sample Newsletter Questionnaire, Table 4B; and Data Entry Spreadsheet, Visitor Survey, Table 5.

Coding is based largely on common sense. The choices you make about types of codes will stem from the format of the questions you have drafted. Examining coding may encourage you to rethink and revise your question formats. This is a very circular process.

Carefully consider the goals of your study and determine the level of detail you need to extract. If you need to distinguish 18-year-olds from 21-year-olds, you will want to code the age data differently than if you only want to distinguish those under 40 from those over 40 years of age.

CODING TYPES

Sample Newsletter Questionnaire, Table 4A, refers to the Getty Museum's newsletter survey and illustrates the project manager's primary role in coding: transferral of the coding for tabulation and analysis to an actual questionnaire so someone else can do the actual work of tabulating each response on each questionnaire. Table 4B incorporates two standard conventions: numbers in parentheses indicate column numbers on your spreadsheet; numbers without parentheses indicate actual code numbers or values which are entered into the columns and which represent responses. At the upper right corner of both tables, there is a code "ID(1-2)." This indicates that columns (1) and (2) on Table 5 identify the respondent. The number of columns you need for this identification depends on the number of ways in which you want to track your respondents. For example, we tracked ours with a survey number [column (1)] and a one-letter code representing their geographic region [column (2)].

There are several types of codes. Typically more than one type of code will be used on a questionnaire. Each type is described below and illustrated on the Coded Master Sheet, Table 4B.

Factual or listing codes are used when a question allows for the selection of more than one response. In Question 1 on Table 4B, each possible response (Alone, With my spouse or partner, etc.) is given a separate column; the possible coding numerals within each column are "1" for "selected" and "O" for "did not select." To record the coded data, Question 1 requires seven columns on Table 5 (columns 9). Note that every time we have a question in this format, we used "O" to represent "did not select" and "1" for "selected." This consistency or standardization of coding responses helped us detect errors and analyze the results later.

Bracket codes assign a category to a range of numbers as in Question 2, Table 4B. Each response is assigned one number. Unless you have more than nine response choices, there is no response assigned a two-digit number; only one column on Table 5 is needed. It is important to note that we have provided a numerical code to indicate "no response." The same number should be used for "no response" in each question (commonly, "O" or "9"). This consistency helps the coders and increases the accuracy of the data. Question 3 illustrates a series of bracket codes.

Reason codes are used for open-ended questions where no clear-cut set of responses exists, as in Question 3, column 18, which codes the query, "What other information would you like to see covered in the Calendar? (Please write in.)" The challenge here is to deal with numerous ideas in one response.

There are several sensible methods for coding these textual responses; the choice depends on the goals of your study. Under some circumstances, it may be appropriate to make a list of anticipated answers and compare them with the data you collected. Are the responses you predicted really the ones you got? Or are there other responses that should be added to or deleted from your list? After modifying your list, compare it again until you feel comfortable that the categories of responses you have established accurately reflect the thoughts people expressed.

Another useful method which avoids the potential limitations of preconceived responses is to collect your data first and then look through about 20% of your completed surveys, but no fewer than 50 surveys total. Record key words or phrases and keep a running tally of how often each appears. Try to group these responses into meaningful categories. Next, ask someone else to review the same questionnaires. See if he or she comes up with the same key words and categories. By reworking this coding scheme until you reach consensus, you stand a better chance of arriving at categories of information that will be most useful to the decision makers and of translating visitor responses into language that will have implications for change. Finally, assign a number to each category, as with the bracket or factual coded responses. This is the method we chose for setting up our coded questionnaire for the Getty Museum newsletter survey; our list of key words appears beneath Question 3, Table 4B.

Limit the number of coded responses to six or seven. Opt to code more responses and you will end up with a laundry list of responses and an incredibly challenging analysis task. (Some sources recommend as few as two or three; we limited our example to five.) If you encounter more than six ideas in one free-form response, you might want to code just the first six, unless the purpose of your study dictates that you search for several particular key phrases. If so, flag those responses as the most important and only code them.

Field codes can be used for numerical data, including age, income, zip codes, and number of visits. The response is coded exactly as given, as in Question 4, Table 4B. Using a field code allows you to capture the most detailed amount of data possible without any extra time or effort. The data can be easily categorized later if you find collapsing them with similar data are more useful. Generally, one column is sufficient.

Pattern codes allow for combinations of responses. In Question 5, Table 4A, we were particularly interested in isolating those individuals who knew about the lecture and concert programs but who did not attend, that is, the "Yes/No" respondents. We combined the responses to the two questions into one code which lets us examine those respondents separately; we can look at the differences among the groups that responded they were "Aware of, but did not attend, "Aware of and did attend," or "Not aware of and did not attend."

CODING INCORRECT OR INCOMPLETE RESPONSES

No matter how carefully you word your questionnaire, some people will not follow the instructions. Here are some common errors and suggested remedies.

If respondents choose two or more responses when they should have selected only one, many times you can garner information from the rest of the questionnaire that will suggest one answer as more accurate than the others. For example, our visitor survey asked the following two questions:

- If you have completed college or graduate school, which of the following fields best describes your academic major? (Choose one response.)

What is your occupation or chief activity?

Predictably, we ended up with a number of completed surveys which indicated, for example, business and humanities as academic majors. Because we needed one response, we checked those majors against the current occupation and chose the one most closely associated. This is certainly not foolproof, but is often preferable to throwing out the question and response.

In other situations, however, you will simply have to count the incorrect answer as a "no response." For example, if the respondent checks both "Male" and "Female" for "Sex," "No response" is the appropriate assignment.

If a question is left blank, this should usually be coded as a "no response. On occasion, however, another assignment will be appropriate. For example, in our question about academic majors, we had a response option, "Does not apply to me." If the question was left blank and it was clear from a previous response that the person did not attend college, we coded it as "Does not apply to me."

Sometimes a respondent will write in his own reply rather than selecting from the responses you have provided. This can often be avoided by providing the "Other" category. Again, if necessary, you can choose the given response that most closely approximates the respondent's written-in response.

WHO PERFORMS THE CODING?

This is a very important consideration. Poorly coded and/or entered data can be both time-consuming and costly to correct. Even worse, that data can cause you and the other stakeholders in the survey to lose faith in the results, jeopardizing the effort.

If your budget allows, hire professional coders and data entry personnel. University computing centers, local business or secretarial schools and referrals from other arts or marketing organizations are good sources. Typically they charge either by the hour or by the keystroke. The number of keystrokes in your questionnaire is roughly the same as the number of columns on your data entry sheet times the number of anticipated respondents.) You can save keystrokes and money by setting up the column titles yourself. Otherwise, add additional money for programming. Professional coders can provide an estimate if they have a copy of the questionnaire and a sample of the way you would like your finished data entry spreadsheet to look.

Be sure to ask professional coders about their ability to verify. Verification is a feature of most data entry software that allows for the checking of data to minimize errors. One person enters the data in the entry mode. A second person enters it again in a verify mode in which the computer compares this second set of data to the first and alerts the operator of discrepancies. This is a very important feature and is usually included in the data entry price.

If you are evaluating on a shoestring, volunteers, temporary workers, or support staff can be used to code and enter the data. Bear in mind, though coding and data entry are not difficult; they are tedious, time-consuming and prone to error. The coders should have large blocks of uninterrupted time (e.g., no telephones to answer), the patience to check their work and should be available throughout the duration of the project. This continuity is essential; a coder can quickly memorize the codes and will become faster and more accurate. You do not want to continually retrain coders.

WHAT ARE THE CODERS ACTUALLY DOING?

Using your Coded Master Sheet, the coders physically write the appropriate code and column numbers on the completed questionnaires. Next, they (or someone else) enter the data on a computer or manual data entry spreadsheet. Separating coding from data entry is the most reliable method, as the coders can concentrate on their single task.

Or the coders can look at the completed questionnaires and, without actually writing the code numbers on the questionnaires, enter the numbers into the data entry sheet spreadsheet. This is the faster method because a step is eliminated; however, it is more difficult to check the work of the coder because the potential for coding error is now combined with the potential for typing error. A feasible compromise is to have the coders physically write codes for some of the more difficult or complicated questions (like the bracket and reason codes) and then enter the others directly.

WORKING WITH CODERS

Whether you use in-house or professional coders, make them feel an integral part of the survey project. Give them the background of the study, its purposes and the reasons for its design. If in-house staff is used, have one or more practice sessions where the principles of coding are carefully explained and coders can practice coding several completed questionnaires. As project manager, you should check their work on the spot and discuss and resolve any areas of confusion. Do not be afraid to revise the codes at this stage. The fresh eyes of the coders may very well reveal some possible answers which you overlooked. Professional coders will no doubt have helpful suggestions for revising question formats to make the coding and analysis jobs easier.

When using in-house coders, you, as the project manager or another person involved in the design of the coding sheet should conduct random checks on the accuracy of the data. Recode the first ten questionnaires that each coder completes. Seeing their errors will help highlight areas that need further clarification. Gradually reduce the number of surveys you recode to approximately 10 % of the total. Again, let the goals of the survey dictate your actions. If there are a few questions that are particularly difficult to code and are essential to the results, you may want to recode or check all of them.

ANALYZING THE DATA

by Randi Korn

Reprinted from *Visitor Surveys: A User's Manual*, American Association of Museums, 1990, 69-78.

With your field work completed, you have collected a wealth of data that will help you make decisions about your programs. Still, a major job remains—the conversion of this raw data into something meaningful. Three basic steps make up the process: coding the data, entering the data, and analyzing the data.

The analysis of data described in this section is no more complicated than tasks you do every day on your job. Do you keep track of how many students take your "Introduction to the Museum" tour? Your "How to Look at the Collections" tour? Can you determine what percentage of all students took each tour? If yes, then you can easily handle this chapter, which presents some of the most basic ways of beginning to get a feel for what your data reveals. With this chapter, we hope you will learn some slightly more complicated techniques and will acquire the vocabulary necessary to discuss analysis with an outside statistician. You can get your feet wet, but you cannot master swimming using only these techniques and information.

There are a number of useful statistical analysis methods that can reveal significant things about your data. Practically speaking, these methods require that you have access to a statistical software package (like SAS, SPSS, or CRUNCH). If you can engage free or for a fee the services of someone skilled in statistical analysis, please do so. Someone with those skills may already have been involved during your question-writing and pretesting phases. Check with local universities or community colleges to find students skilled in statistical analysis. Or, if your budget permits, contact a consultant. A referral from another museum or similar organization is usually a reliable source. The time and effort you have invested warrants as thorough an understanding of the results as you can obtain.

Again, if your budget allows, you can turn the data over to your statistician, or someone with whom he or she feels comfortable, for entry directly into a statistical software package. For our purposes with the Getty Museum Visitor Survey, however, we chose to enter our own data into a data entry spreadsheet, perform some preliminary analysis ourselves and then have the data transferred and translated, or "imported," to a statistical package by our statistician.

This helped in two ways. We saved a fair amount of money by handling the data entry ourselves. And, by manipulating the data a little bit on our own, we were better able to articulate some of the relationships we were interested in exploring. For example, we had hypothesized that there would be fairly strong differences between our summer visitors and those who came in the fall or winter. We quickly discovered that we were wrong and were able to eliminate a whole series of analyses from our statistician's docket.

MANUAL TALLIES

If you have a rather small sample (less than 100) and fewer than ten or so questions, manual tallies of the responses may serve your purposes just as well as computerized analysis, although your analysis will take longer. The Manual Tally Sheet, Visitor Survey, Table 6 (page 40), indicates the response categories in the left-hand column and tick marks beside each category indicate the number of people providing that response. In the right-hand column, the responses are totaled. This table shows frequency distributions, one of the many points discussed in this chapter that can be performed manually with some success.

ENTERING DATA WITH SPREADSHEETS

Spreadsheets are frequently used for financial functions within U.S. museums. Although spreadsheets are not designed specifically for statistical analysis, its many features lend themselves well to deriving some basic information which can be sorted and manipulated in a variety of ways without time-consuming manual tracking. Most other spreadsheet or statistical software packages can be applied to your survey too.

Please refer to Table 5, Data Entry Spreadsheet. We have a key tip to share. In columns (20) and (21), we might have chosen to place the labels for lecture programs and concert programs on two rows as follows:

LECT	CNCRT
PROGS	PROGS

The bottom row in each label reads "PROGS." You will see later that this is problematic, for as you extract data only your lowest row of labels will be visible. "PROGS" would not distinguish between lecture or concert. The lowest row of your column descriptions must be meaningful and unique. Do not repeat column descriptions in the bottom row because that gives the computer a mixed message. You must begin entering your data in the row immediately below the labels row. Do not leave a blank row.

BASIC ANALYSIS TECHNIQUES

Here we sometimes choose not to explain the calculations of each analysis method, but instead emphasize the usefulness of each method. When the function can easily be performed on a spreadsheet, it is noted with the basic command.

DESCRIPTIVE ANALYSIS

These first four methods are used to describe the results of your sample. Frequency distributions offer an easy and meaningful way to get a preliminary handle on your data. The result is a list of the response options with either the number of people who provided each response or the percentage of people doing so, or both. For example, looking at Table 5, Question 1 summarizes like this:

	SELECTED	DID NOT SELECT
Visit alone	3–60 %	2–40 %
Visit with spouse	2–40 %	3–60 %
Visit with friends	2–40 %	3–60 %
Visit with children < 16	0 %	5–100 %
Visit with children > 16	2–40 %	3–60 %
Visit with other family members	0–0 %	5–100 %
Visit as part of a tour group	2–40 %	3–60 %

Arithmetic mean is obtained by adding up all the responses for a given question and dividing that total by the number of responses. For example, in Question 4 on Table 4A, we asked respondents to write in their age. On Table 5, adding up that column of responses [(19) Age] gives us a total of 220 and dividing by five (the given number of respondents), we have a mean age of 44.

Use the mean when your responses are normally distributed, that is, when they generally form a bell curve. To determine whether or not your responses are normally distributed, take a piece of graph paper and plot them. (For these graphs we have assumed many more respondents than we have shown in previous examples.) In the following, the X or horizontal axis represents the age of the respondents; the Y or vertical axis represents the number of respondents who provided that age. You can see that in the first example, the responses form roughly a bell curve. In the second, however, there are many more younger people represented than older. It would be misleading to calculate an average age for the group, as it would be affected by a very small number of extreme ages. In this case, a median would be more accurate.

The median is the value midway between the highest and lowest values in a group. It is less affected by extreme values than is the mean and is, therefore, sometimes considered to be a more reliable measure. In Question 4 on Table 5, 40 is the median age because 50 % of the responses lie above it (61 and 54) and 50 % lie below it (29 and 36).

Standard deviation is a measurement of the homogeneity or variability of data. In our original age category (Question 4, Table 5), we had the following ages: 54, 36, 61, 29, and 40. The median age was 40 and the mean

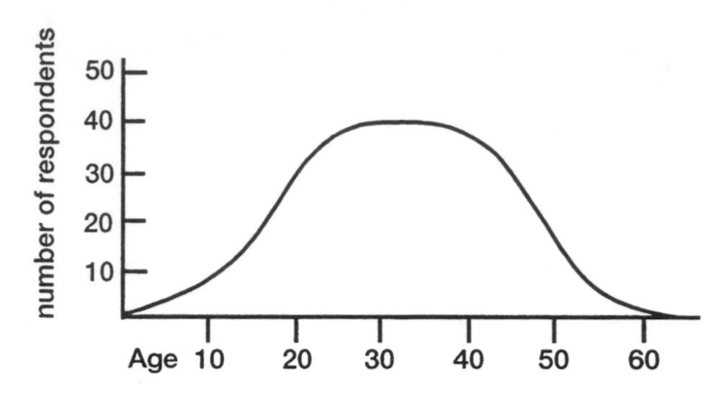

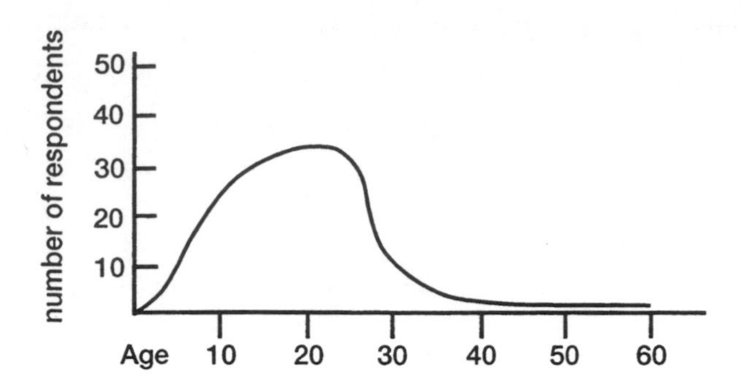

First Sample of people

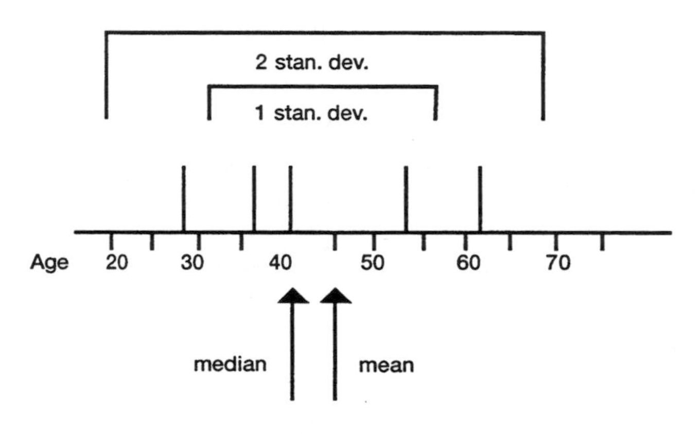

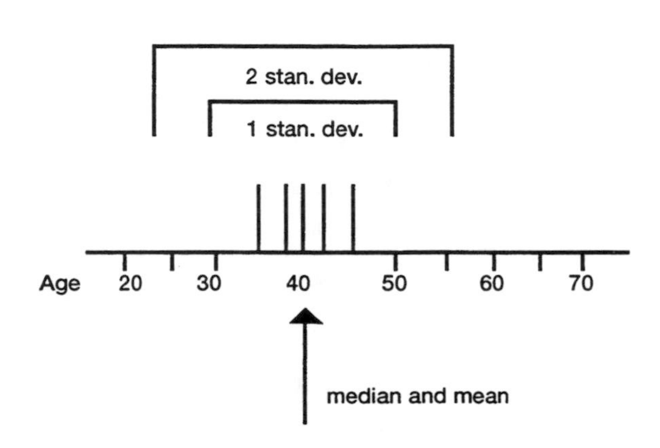

Second sample of people

was 44. Perhaps we want to compare our sample with that of another museum in town that was conducting a similar study. Both their median and mean age were 40, but the figures they recorded were 35, 40, 38, 42, and 45. Although examining the median age indicates that these groups are identical with respect to age, eyeballing the data clearly reveals that the second sample is much more closely clustered.

The standard deviation of the first sample is 11.78 (a calculation we won't get into) which means that about 68 % of all responses are expected to fall within 11.78 (or nearly 12) on either side of the mean. (Sixty-eight is a scientifically-established percentage for one standard deviation.) You would, therefore, expect 68 % of all ages in the sample to be roughly between 32 and 56 (44-12 = 32; 44 + 12 = 56). About 95 % of the responses are expected to fall within two standard deviations (12 + 12 = 24), or between 20 and 68 (44-24 = 20; 44 + 24 = 68).

The second sample exhibits quite a different range. The standard deviation is 7.6 (or around 8), the mean is 40, so we would expect 68 % of all age responses to be between about 32 and 48, and 95 % to fall between 24 and 56. The age range represented by the first group is much broader than that of the second group.

COMPARATIVE ANALYSIS

Comparative analysis methods are used to examine relationships between pieces of data. Spreadsheets provide little assistance for comparative analysis. Using a fictitious scenario, suppose we were interested in learning if the respondents' family income affects how frequently they visit the museum. Our hypothesis might be that members of families with higher incomes tend to visit alone more frequently. We are looking for a relationship that may shed some light on who visits frequently. Therefore, this is our dependent variable. That is, frequency of visitation is dependent upon something; we suggest it may be family income. Income is the independent variable.

	< $20K	$20-29	$30	$40-49	$50-75	$75 +	NA
First time	20%	30%	40%	10%	0%	0%	0%
1 other time	30%	50%	0%	10%	10%	0%	0%
2-3 times	10%	10%	20%	40%	20%	0%	0%
4-6 times	10%	0%	10%	50%	20%	10%	0%
7 + times	0%	0%	5%	40%	45%	0%	0%

Family Income

Crosstabulation or "crosstabs" allow you to show the relationship between independent and dependent variables by setting up a simple table. The dependent variable (frequency of visitation during the last two years) appears down the left-hand column, while the independent variable (income) is listed across the top of the table.

The above table tells us that, of those people who attended the museum one other time during the last two years, 80% (30% plus 50%) have family incomes under $29,000. Of those who attended seven or more times, 95% had incomes of $40,000 or more. Although the data are fictitious and the example somewhat simplistic, this example demonstrates how useful this kind of table can be in testing your planning team's theories about your visitors.

Statistical packages such as those mentioned earlier will produce these tables automatically for you, once you design and enter the categories and the data, relieving you of the trials of drawing tables and calculating percentages.

Chi-square (pronounced ky-square) is a statistical formula used to determine whether or not a significant relationship exists between two crosstabulated variables. It neither determines the strength of that relationship nor proves that one variable causes another. Chi-square is used when you know the value of one variable and you want to be able to predict the value of another variable.

Suppose that in our above example, we had found that there indeed seemed to be a relationship between family income and frequency of visitation. (Our fictitious data did seem to indicate such a relationship.) We would want to use a chi-square test to uncover the significance of that relationship. Does high family income only hint at tendencies to visit frequently or does it quite reliably predict it? If a relationship is significant, it is very unlikely that the differences between groups of visitors (those who came frequently and those who did not, for example) occurred by chance; in other words, it is likely that those differences actually did occur in the population from which the sample was drawn. Our goal here is to be able to predict how frequently a group will visit the museum by knowing its family income.

You and your statistician will want to discuss the "level of significance" you choose. A common level is .05, referred to as the "p" or probability value. This means that there is a 95% probability (1 minus .05 = .95 or 95%) that the relationship being explored exists; that is, in 95 out of 100 cases, there really would be a relationship between family income and frequency of visitation. Likewise, there is a 5% chance that the relationship does not exist; or in five out of 100 cases, a relationship we had assumed was due purely to chance.

If you have a very large sample, there is a greater chance of uncovering relatively unimportant relationships simply because you are looking at a wider cross-section of cases. You should choose a level of significance that is smaller, like .01. Then there is only a 1% probability that the relationship explored does not exist and is due to chance.

If you have two samples and therefore two means, you can determine whether the differences between those means are significant by using a t-test. In our earlier age example, we had two populations and two means, 44 and 40. Based on this information alone, we really cannot determine whether the differences between these means are statistically significant. That is, are the two populations under examination really different or are these means close enough to indicate that they are quite similar? If we get a t-test result that is significant at the .01 level, we know that there is only a 1% probability that the difference in the means is due to chance. The 1% probability level provides a high level of confirmation of a real difference between the two groups.

The goal of regression analysis is to explain one dependent variable by one (simple regression) or more (multiple regression) independent variables. For example, you might theorize that people who do not like to read interpretive explanations of works of art (e.g., labels) are well-educated, high income, college art history majors who have traveled abroad extensively. You would look for a regression equation in which family income, propensity for travel, educational level and field of study accurately predict a like or dislike of interpretive labels.

An it-squared figure is part of a regression analysis and indicates how much of your dependent variable is explained by the independent variables. An it-squared result of .998 indicates that 99.8% of a person's like or dislike of interpretive materials can be explained by family income, educational background, etc.

An understanding of these basic analysis methods will enable you to grasp some preliminary results on your own (especially by using frequency distributions) and to make intelligent decisions, in conjunction with a statistician, about probing more deeply into your data.

Of course, in the end, all analysis comes down to the practical question, What does this mean for us? Do we really care whether the median age of our audience differs from our neighbor's by four years? Although we may not care about a four-year difference, perhaps we would consider a difference of eight years to be important. It all depends on what information is important enough for your institution to form the basis for its decisions and changes.

USING THE DATA

by Randi Korn

Reprinted from *Visitor Surveys: A User's Manual*, American Association of Museums, 1990, 69-78.

In our opinion, this is the most crucial stage of the audience survey process. You have invested time, money, and a lot of effort into finding out about your visitors. Your underlying goal has always been to use the information as a decision-making tool and to make changes that will benefit both the visitor and your organization. Now that you have this information, how can you make sure it is used in that way?

REPORTING THE FINDINGS

You can report the results of your survey in written or verbal form. A combination of the two proved effective for us.

Verbal presentations can be either formal or informal. With the Getty Museum Visitor Survey, we first presented the results to the planning team, but did not encourage discussion at that time. This presentation was followed by a written report. A series of staff meetings, set to specifically address the results of the visitor survey, became lively discussion forums for the whole education staff. In each session, one general inquiry and its resulting data were considered in detail. What ramifications did the data have for the programs and services we offered? What did it tell us about the interests of our visitors? How should we change our offerings to meet those needs?

These discussion formats were designed to encourage involvement from all staff members who may be affected by potential changes. They offered the opportunity to discuss details of the findings, explore new ideas, brainstorm, and consider staff actions in relationship to the audience.

In verbal presentations, visual aids like handouts of charts, graphs, transparencies, and slides are useful for describing results. Focus on patterns in the data-on what the data means. While it is important to present some of the relevant numbers, avoid inundating your audience with percentages and proportions. Highlight those areas of the findings that have clear implications for your programs: trends in attendance, attitudes towards your institution, demographic shifts in your audience makeup.

Written reports are essential to detail the purpose, inquiries, methodologies, sampling procedures, analysis methods, and results of your survey. This is your opportunity to be thorough and complete in your descriptions. This document will be used for reference. Strive to find a balance between technical jargon and omission of information. Write clearly and explain difficult concepts using examples. Here again, help the reader focus on patterns in the data. Do not assume that your readers understand statistical concepts.

We suggest you have a volunteer type up responses to the open-ended questions you may have had on your survey and include that list of responses in the appendix of your final report. We found that many people took the opportunity to comment on aspects of our institution about which we had not specifically asked. Their insights, while not quantifiably significant, were revealing and interesting.

ANALYSIS VERSUS INTERPRETATION

Analysis uncovers relationships within the data and serves to describe your sample. Interpretation highlights the meaning of the results; the implications they have for you and your organization. It should be the job of the planning committee (and other staff members you may choose to involve in the discussions) to derive this meaning from the results. The inclusion of interpretation in either a written or verbal report is open for debate. Because each person will interpret the results from a different perspective, applying his/her own frame of reference, your own interpretation can, at best, serve as a guideline for discussion. It is your responsibility, as project manager, to facilitate this interpretation by asking, "What does this information mean to us?"

Responses to many of your survey questions will not surprise you. They will support earlier hunches and can add impetus to plans for changes and modifications in programs or services. More difficult, however, are responses which do not support your perception of your audience. This information may not be pleasant to hear and is more difficult to impart to the decision makers. This is your opportunity to reemphasize the fact that this research was done with the intention of making changes, not simply to reaffirm that your institution is doing a good job.

KEEPING THE MOMENTUM GOING

With your decision makers, list by priority the changes your museum hopes to implement. Put someone in charge of each project. Set a timetable and a schedule for making progress reports. Allow ample time for the interesting discussions that will be stimulated, but do not let the ball drop there. At the Getty Museum, the director has appointed a committee to examine the results from the two studies mentioned here, plus a number of smaller studies done over the last two years. The committee's goal is to make recommendations to the director about changes that should be made throughout the museum. It is composed of an interesting mixture of staff members from curatorial, education, security, and public information departments.

If a particularly interesting facet emerges from your first study, one your institution would like to explore further, do a follow-up study. A follow-up study can stretch your existing investment in research.

Do share the results of your study with all staff members, paid and unpaid. It is important for everyone at your institution to understand the high priority being placed on understanding the characteristics, attitudes, and behaviors of your visitors: who they are, where they have been, and where they are going.

Through your persistence and enthusiasm, the results of your study can affect the operations and philosophy of your organization for years to come. Make this survey process a part of all your planning activities. You may find that a survey will prompt your institution to conduct some visitor evaluation studies to determine why visitors are pleased or displeased with a particular program. Do they understand gallery talks? Are the talks meeting their needs? As you begin to integrate an assessment of your activities into your usual routine, you will find that the results of each new study are enhanced by the findings of those that have gone before. The returns on investment truly multiply.

FROM THE J. PAUL GETTY MUSEUM EXPERIENCE:

Staff members at the J. Paul Getty Museum were quite surprised when a visitor survey revealed that 74% of the visitors had visited the museum only once in the last two years (including the current visit), and only 26% had visited the Museum more than once in the last two years. At this time, staff members in the education department were in the process of reexamining the topics of the gallery talks, and the discussion centered on the fact that there was not a "highlights of the Museum" or an "orientation" to the Museum" talk, even though 74% of the visitors were not frequent visitors. The gallery talks tended to focus on one of the collection areas. Visitor survey results indicated that while the visiting public was highly educated, it was not very knowledgeable about art. Only approximately 10% of the visitors had taken any art history classes in college and fewer had majored in it.

These figures convinced staff members to reexamine the topics and content of the gallery talks. As the discussions continued, staff members suggested several topics in light of the visitor profile, determined by the visitor survey. The results of the visitor survey sparked the curiosity of staff members. They asked themselves, "How do we know if the gallery talks we are proposing would be attended by visitors?" This worthwhile question was answered by conducting a simple, informal survey of visitor reactions to a variety of gallery talks. The details of the study are not important here, but the fact that the results caused staff members to reconsider their standard approach to planning gallery talks is significant. They began to understand that visitor behaviors and reactions can be useful when planning visitor programs.

TABLE 4A: SAMPLE NEWSLETTER QUESTIONNAIRE ID (1-2)

1. I usually visit the J. Paul Getty Museum: (You may circle more than one.)
   [ ] Alone
   [ ] With my spouse or partner
   [ ] With friends
   [ ] With children under 16
   [ ] With children over 16
   [ ] With other family members
   [ ] As part of an organized tour

2. My total current family income is:
   [ ] Under $20,000
   [ ] $20,000 - $29,999
   [ ] $30,000 - $39,999
   [ ] $40,000 - $49,999
   [ ] $50,000 - $75,000
   [ ] Over $75,000

3. I am interested in information about: (Please circle A for Very Interested, B for Somewhat Interested, or C for Not Interested.)

VERY INTERESTED	SOMEWHAT INTERESTED	NOT INTERESTED	
A	B	C	General news about the Museum
A	B	C	Evening concerts and lectures
A	B	C	Lists of Getty publications
A	B	C	Guest scholar activities
A	B	C	Programs for students
A	B	C	Recent acquisitions
A	B	C	Current or new exhibitions

   What other information would you like to see covered in the *Calendar*? (Please write in.) ____________________.

4. My age is ____________.

5. Are you aware of the Getty Museum evening lecture and concert series?

NO	YES	
______	______	Lectures
______	______	Concerts

   Have you attended evening lectures or concerts at the Getty Museum in the past year?

NO	YES	
______	______	Lectures
______	______	Concerts

TABLE 4B: CODED MASTER SHEET FOR SAMPLE NEWSLETTER QUESTIONNAIRE ID(1-2)

FACTUAL OR LISTING CODES

1. I usually visit the J. Paul Getty Museum: (You may circle more than one.)

(3) [ ] Alone
(4) [ ] With my spouse or partner
(5) [ ] With friends
(6) [ ] With children under 16
(7) [ ] With children over 16
(8) [ ] With other family members
(9) [ ] As part of an organized tour

1 = SELECTED
0 = DID NOT SELECT

(10) 2. My total current family income is:

1 [ ] Under $20,000
2 [ ] $20,000 - $29,999
3 [ ] $30,000 - $39,999
4 [ ] $40,000 - $49,999
5 [ ] $50,000 - $75,000
6 [ ] Over $75,000

0 = NO RESPONSE

3. I am interested in information about: (Please circle A for Very Interested, B for Somewhat Interested, or C for Not Interested.)

0 = NO RESPONSE

	1 VERY INTERESTED	2 SOMEWHAT INTERESTED	3 NOT INTERESTED	
(11)	A	B	C	General news about the Museum
(12)	A	B	C	Evening concerts and lectures
(13)	A	B	C	Lists of Getty publications
(14)	A	B	C	Guests scholar activities
(15)	A	B	C	Programs for students
(16)	A	B	C	Recent acquisitions
(17)	A	B	C	Current or new exhibitions

REASON CODES

(18) What other information would you like to see covered in the *Calendar*? (Please write in.) ____________________.

KEY WORDS: 1. BRENTWOOD FACILITY; 2. DIRECTOR'S COMMENTS; 3. IN-DEPTH ART HISTORY ARTICLES; 4. CAREER OPPORTUNITIES; 5. VOLUNTEER OPPORTUNITIES
0 = NO RESPONSE

FIELD CODES

(19) 4. My age is ____________. 0 = NO RESPONSE

PATTERN CODES

5. Are you aware of the Getty Museum evening lecture and concert series?

NO	YES	
______	______	Lectures
______	______	Concerts

Have you attended evening lectures or concerts at the Getty Museum in the past year?

NO	YES	
______	______	Lectures
______	______	Concerts

(20) (21)
LECTURES / CONCERTS
0 = NO RESPONSE
1 = YES / YES
2 = YES / NO
3 = NO / NO

TABLE 5: DATA ENTRY SPREADSHEET, VISITOR SURVEY

TABLE 5: DATA ENTRY SPREADSHEET – VISITOR SURVEY

(1)	(2)	(3)	(4)	(5)	(6)	(7)	(8)	(9)	(10)	(11)	(12)	(13)	(14)	(15)	(16)	(17)	(18)	(19)	(20)	(21)
ID	Q1-Visit with								Q2 3-Info									Q4	Q5	
#	GEO CD	ALONE	SPSE	FRNDS	<16	>16	OTHER	TOUR	INCOME	NEWS	CN/LCT	PUBS	SCHLR	STDNT	ACQU	EXHIB	OTHER	AGE	LECT	CNCRT
101	L	0	1	1	0	1	0	1	2	2	1	0	3	2	1	1	2	54	0	1
102	C	1	0	0	0	0	0	0	4	3	3	2	3	2	1	1	3	36	2	1
103	L	1	0	0	0	0	0	0	4	1	3	2	1	2	1	2	5	61	3	2
104	L	0	1	1	0	0	0	1	0	1	2	3	0	3	1	1	0	29	1	0
105	U	1	0	0	0	1	0	0	5	2	1	2	1	3	1	2	1	40	1	2

58

NOTE: Done in Lotus 1-2-3.
Columns show each coded response from each questionnaire.
The number (1-21) on the top row indicate column numbers that are cross-referenced to the Coded Master Sheet.
The second row shows the question number, and the third row indicates the response options.

TABLE 6: MANUAL TALLY SHEET, VISITOR SURVEY

QUESTION # 1 : I usually visit the Museum:

Response	Number of People Providing Response	Total
Alone	III	3
w/ spouse/partner	II	2
w/ friends	II	2
w/ children under 16		0
w/ children over 16	II	2
w/ other family		0
w/ organized tour	II	2

CHAPTER 3

Front-End Evaluation: What Do Visitors Know and How Do They Feel About Your Exhibition or Program Topic

FRONT-END EVALUATION: A TOOL FOR EXHIBIT AND PROGRAM PLANNING

Minda Borun

Paper of the same title presented at the annual meeting of the American Association of Museums, Denver, Colorado, May 1991.

Front-end evaluation is a procedure for finding out visitors' knowledge, ideas, and feelings about a planned exhibition or program. The process begins with the development of a preliminary conceptual outline or topic to be treated. A sample of visitors is interviewed to explore their thoughts about this subject. What information do they already have and what are the widespread misconceptions which block further understanding?

Results of the front-end study inform the modification of the exhibit's outline and planned components, so that critical problem areas are addressed and the exhibit can speak to novice as well as expert visitors. Without such analysis, exhibitions are often far too complex for the average visitor. This is the most critical phase of exhibit or program assessment and planning. It sets the starting point, boundaries, and levels of discourse. In contrast to formative evaluation, front-end studies are preventive as opposed to corrective.

PREREQUISITES FOR FRONT-END STUDY

Even before the front-end study, you will need to do a standard demographic and psychographic survey of your museum visitors. (See reference 1.) This survey tells you who's coming to the museum, why and when, and with what goals and expectations. Such studies should be done periodically to keep up with changes in the composition of the museum audience. Once the basic survey is done, you can move on to front-end analysis for your specific project. You are seeking answers to two kinds of questions.

Affective—How interested are people in the overall subject and possible subtopics which may be included? Which of several alternative approaches, titles, themes, subtopics, and treatments is most appealing?

Cognitive—What do people know and what relevant misconceptions do they have about the topic to be treated?

NAIVE NOTIONS AND LEARNING

Before detailing the steps involved in conducting a front-end evaluation, I will focus on the importance of understanding visitors' misconceptions as part of a new view of the learning process. The following are examples of such misconceptions.

"Painstaking detail is the mark of true excellence in painting."

"The Greeks and Romans are responsible for all of civilization."

"Dinosaurs lived at the same time as cavemen".

These are all incorrect beliefs which are widely shared by "novices" or non-experts in art history, history, and paleontology, respectively.

Cognitive scientists view learning as a transition from novice to expert within a field of knowledge. Generally, the findings indicate that there are differences in the concepts each group uses to think about the field and the way those concepts are structured. So it's not the case that novices have no conceptions about a subject; they are not blank slates -rather their ideas are different from those of experts. (See references 2,3,4,5.)

Studies of elementary and middle school (See references 6,7.) through high school and college (See references 8,9,10.) indicate that students enter the classroom with preconceived notions about the world. Both cognitive psychologists and science educators have contributed to a body of literature on what has been variously termed "naive knowledge," "alternative frameworks or schemata,""preconceptions," and "misconceptions."

Learners, whether adults or children, students, or museum visitors, are not empty vessels to be filled with information. Instead, they form their own ideas on how the world works. Their theories tend to combine limited observations or phenomena with intuitive explanations and misinterpreted instruction. But, ideas that seem to be true based on limited observation and intuition are often incomplete or inaccurate. Naive notions of a concept can be creative, seem sensible, and yet prove to contain significant elements which are incorrect.

These common sense or "naive notions" are not associated with developmental stages. They are held as well by children; they are deeply rooted and difficult to change. Further, these notions are highly consistent from one person to the next and tend to persist in spite of conflicting information presented in formal learning situations. (See reference 11.) Research findings about widespread misconceptions have important implications for exhibit-based learning. If we don't uncover and explicitly address visitors' naive notions, exhibits will be interpreted through a filter of pre-existing misconceptions and the exhibit's message will be distorted or missed. (See reference 12.)

It's very important to understand that naive notions are:

- Very widely shared (i.e. often held by over 50% of the population)
- Common among adults as well as children
- Intelligent, common sense notions

FRONT-END EVALUATION PROCESS

With this new perspective on learning, we can now return to the process of front-end evaluation. The following are the steps involved in a front-end evaluation.

1. Determine Goals and Objectives

At initial meetings, the museum staff may be involved in heated debate about a project's goals. Those responsible for exhibit design, education, public programs, development, and marketing each bring their own goals to the table. The task here is to acknowledge that there are multiple goals, each of which must be clearly defined and then translated into measurable objectives. Objectives specify what people will do or say if the goal is achieved. For a front-end evaluation study, cognitive or learning goals are often of prime importance.

2. Create a Content Outline

The next step is to identify the main ideas associated with your topic. Also important are specifying the technical words and standard teaching tools (e.g. graphs, charts, diagrams, formulas) generally used to teach the subject. These will be tried out on visitors to see if they are understood, need to be defined or explained, or are too difficult to use.

3. Select a Data Collection Strategy

Here the study is designed. First, the data gathering instrument and procedure must be pilot tested and revised. It's hard to know what questions to ask; the first round of questions needs to be exploratory. Ask people to define or explain the subject in their own words. Once people's thinking patterns begin to become clear, a more structured procedure can be used.

We specify the techniques which will be used to assess audience response and develop appropriate measuring instruments. Techniques include structured surveys, in-depth interviews, and group discussions (focus groups). Instruments include questionnaires, open-ended interviews, and various kinds of quizzes. Questionnaires can use different sorts of questions: open-ended, fill-in, multiple choice, matching, rating scales, and statement agreement, to name a few.

These are all different ways to determine what is in people's heads—what they know, think and feel; how they name, categorize and relate ideas. It's best to go after a complex thought in several different ways. The assessment technique(s) selected will depend both on the topic to be treated and on the preferences and expertise of the evaluator and staff.

4. Conduct Audience Interviews

Data-gathering instruments and procedures are applied to a random sample of visitors to assess the audience's information level, working vocabulary, response to standard teaching techniques, common misconceptions, and interests and preferences with regard to the proposed subject. As in all situations involving interviewing visitors, some ethical considerations should be kept in mind and clearly communicated to your subjects. You do not want to make people uncomfortable. You are not testing the visitors, just trying to find out what people like them think in order to make exhibits that will be interesting and helpful. You are asking visitors to become partners in the process of developing a new program. If done tactfully, people are usually pleased to participate in the process.

5. Tabulate and Analyze the Data

Data is put into organized, interpretable form and a summary or report is written. The data are studied to look for patterns of response. Categories of responses are established and the frequency of common responses is tabulated Standard presentation graphics show frequency distributions as bar graphs or pie charts or graphs, showing the incidence of various ideas and reactions.

6. Revise Goals and Content Outline

Instructional goals of the exhibit are now reconsidered in light of the audience's level of knowledge and a new project plan emerges. The visitor's or novice view is compared to the expert view or desired final state. If it seems that visitors have the prerequisite knowledge to understand your intended presentation, a conventional teaching approach can be used. If there is a very large gap between novice and expert, it is probably advisable to rethink the exhibit's instructional goals. If there is some correspondence, but also crucial areas of disagreement, it is important to address problem areas in the exhibit or presentation and to build explicit connections between the novice's current approach and more sophisticated ways of looking at the topic.

BENEFITS OF A FRONT-END EVALUATION

Some of the fundamental problems which lead to poor or unsuccessful exhibits can be avoided through front-end evaluation. Such problems include:

- Using language that is too difficult or technical for the audience (i.e., the level of the exhibit is too high).
- Presenting material which is already well known and familiar (the level of the exhibit is too low).
- Using visual aids or teaching techniques (e.g. charts, graphs, diagrams) which are hard to understand and hinder learning rather that facilitate communication.
- Using language or explanations and demonstrations which reinforce people's misconceptions.

EXAMPLE OF FRONT-END ANALYSIS IN EXHIBIT DEVELOPMENT

The Franklin Institute Science Museum in Philadelphia, developed an exhibit on global warming. The project began with a front-end survey of museum visitors to determine what they know about this subject. The most significant finding of the study was that more than three quarters of the people interviewed (78%) believed that global warming is caused by the ozone hole.

Actually, global warming and the ozone hole are two separate environmental problems. Global warming involves the build-up of carbon dioxide and other gases from fossil fuels and other pollutants which creates a canopy that traps the sun's rays and retains heat. Scientists fear that if this process continues to accelerate, as it has over the last century, global warming will cause broad shifts in climatic zones and threaten our food supply. In addition, it will cause the polar ice caps to melt, water levels to rise, and large areas of inhabited land to be flooded. The ozone hole, on the other hand, is a gap in the protective ozone layer of the stratosphere which increases our exposure to harmful ultraviolet rays from the sun and causes skin cancer.

One reason it is important to separate the two problems is that people tend to think that they can simply cut back on the use of hairspray and other sources of chlorofluorocarbons to solve the global warming problem. While such actions would address the cause of the ozone hole, they would have only minimal impact on global warming.

Before the front-end survey, it had not occurred to the exhibit development staff that people would confuse the two concepts. Interviews revealed that the confusion was dramatic. As a result of the front-end evaluation, a significant section of the exhibit plan was devoted to the difference between global warming and the ozone hole.

CONCLUSIONS

The design of educational presentations needs to begin with what learners already know and use familiar vocabulary and concepts. From there, it is up to the designers' creative imagination to develop an effective, attractive educational exhibit or program. Front-end evaluation and revision is later followed by formative evaluation involving the testing of mock-ups of devices and drafts of other educational materials to ensure their effectiveness in addressing misconceptions and communicating with visitors.

Minda Borun is the director of research and evaluation at the Franklin Institute Science Museum in Philadelphia and chair of the Committee on Audience Research and Evaluation (CARE) of the American Association of Museums. She is also an associate professor in the graduate program in museum education at the University of the Arts in Philadelphia. The author of numerous articles and three monographs on studies of visitor learning in the museum setting, she is an evaluation consultant and conducts workshops on exhibit and program evaluation for museums and informal learning institutions and organizations.

REFERENCES

1. Hood, Marilyn, "Audience Research Helps Informed Decisions, *Visitor Studies: Theory, Research and Practice,* Proceedings of the 1991 Visitor Studies Conference, 4, Steven Bitgood (ed.), Center for Social Design, Jacksonville, AL., 18-23, 1991.

2. Chi, M.T.P., P. Feltovich, and R. Glaser, "Categorization and Representation of Physics Problems by Experts and Novices, *Cognitive Science*, 5, 121-152, 1985.

3. Carey, S. Conceptual Change in Childhood, Cambridge, MA: MIT Press, 1985.

4. Carey, S. "Cognitive Science and Science Education", *American Psychologist*, 41 (10), 1123-1130, 1986.

5. Larkin, J.H., L. McDermott, D.P. Simon, and H.A. Simon, "Models of Competence in Solving Physics Problems," *Cognitive Science*, 4, 317-345, 1980.

6. Nussbaum, J. "Children's Conceptions of the Earth as a Cosmic Body: A Cross-Age Study", *Science Education*, 63 (1), 83-93, 1979.

7. Pines, L.A. & Novak, J.D. "The Interaction of Audio-Tutorial Instruction with Student Prior Knowledge: A Proposed Qualitative Case-Study Methodology," *Science Education*, 69 (2), 1985.

8. Clement, J. "Students' Preconceptions in Introductory Mechanics," *American Journal of Physics*, 50 (1) 1982.

9. McCloskey, M. "Naive Conceptions of Motion", presented at the annual meeting of the American Educational Research Association, New York, March, 1982.

10. McDermott, L.C. "Research on Conceptual Understanding in Mechanics", *Physics Today*, 37, 24-32, 1984.

11. Helm, H. and Novak, J.D., "Misconceptions in Science and Mathematics", Proceedings of the First International Seminar on Misconceptions in Science and Mathematics, Ithaca, NY: Cornell University, 12, 1983.

12. Borun, Minda. "Naive Notions and the Design of Science Museum Exhibits" in *What Research Says about Learning in Science Museums.* Association of Science-Technology Centers, May, 1991.

THE USES OF FOCUS GROUPS IN AUDIENCE RESEARCH

by Rosalyn Rubenstein

Reprinted with permission of the author. Rubenstein, Roslyn. *The Uses of Focus Groups in Audience Research. In Visitor Theory, Research and Practice.* Proceedings of the 1990 Visitor Studies Conference 3, Steven Bitgood (ed.) Jacksonville: Center for Social Design, 1990, 181-187.

In the museum literature, several articles and debates address the issue of approaches and methods of audience research (see references on "method" cited in Screven, 1984). Is one approach or method better than the rest? First, the answer is "no". Second, this is not even the particular question which one should ask, because it is not a question of one better than the other, but rather, choosing the most appropriate approach and method—or combination of methods—to answer the particular research questions and problems. In other words, how can one design the research to get the desired information. Indeed, developing the research design is one of the major challenges of any audience research project. To do this well, the designer of a research project should be familiar with a variety of approaches and methods.

This paper discusses one of the methods which I have used in audience research projects, focus groups, also called focus interviews or focused group interviews. These have been used for a variety of audiences and purposes at several Canadian institutions. I have had success with focus groups in these projects because they did provide results which answered the research questions.

The focus group method is commonly used in commercial or consumer research. However, it is less often associated with museums. Although, both Adams (1983) and Loomis (1987) cites its use in museums, there is no accompanying description in these sources. For this reason, the current chapter provides an overview of focus groups in museum settings. For further information on focus groups the reader is referred to Higgenbotham and Cox (1979).

The chapter will be divided into several parts. The first part gives a general description of the focus group method. Second, the process of a focus group is described by breaking it down into its component parts. Third, examples from case studies are provided to show how focus groups have been used and the sorts of data which emerged from the projects. Finally, conclusions are drawn about the projects to which focus groups are appropriate. The paper also makes reference to aspects of this methodology in consumer market research and revisions which I have made in order to apply the technique to museum audience research.

GENERAL DESCRIPTION OF THE FOCUS GROUP METHOD

Focus groups are a qualitative method of research. They take the form of in-depth discussions with groups of about eight to twelve participants, lasting from one to two hours. Focus groups are led by an experienced and well-trained discussion leader or moderator who follows a guide with topics, probes, and target timings. Participants are encouraged to stick to the discussion topic but to say whatever is on their minds. This loosely structured format allows one to identify the range of audience reactions, attitudes, issues, expectations, and perceptions with respect to the project topic. Because the format is loosely structured, it requires knowledge and rigorous training in order to be used effectively.

DESCRIPTION OF THE FOCUS GROUP PROCESS

THE STUDY GUIDE

A guide, or "study guide," is developed in advance for the focus group sessions which includes, probes, and target timings for each of the session topics. The guides are based on the objectives of the research project, and take the following into account:

> The types of questions are suited to a group or questions which people are happy to answer and discuss in front of other people.

Questions which lend themselves to discussion such as open-ended questions and general probes.

The length of the session or the number of items which can be adequately discussed in a period of one to two hours.

A general format which allows the moderator to facilitate a relaxed, thoughtful, and focused in-depth discussion.

The general format for a session study guide may be described as follows.

First, an icebreaker allows group participants to relax and become acquainted with each other. Second, the moderator introduces the focus of the discussion topic. Third, the guide is setup to allow for topic development. This is crucial. The questions and probes must flow in such a way that in-depth discussion can develop in the session. Finally, the discussion may end with a general request for any additional comments or ideas relevant to the discussion topic.

Sometimes, the discussion part of the session is followed by a brief survey, perhaps to acquire specific demographic information from participants, and sometimes another question or two relevant to the discussion topic. This gives participants the opportunity to answer questions privately and after they have given the issues some thought. An alternative is to hand out surveys at the beginning of a session to obtain information before participants have discussed the issue with the others. While these brief surveys are distributed among participants, the session study guide is seen and used only by the person responsible for leading or moderating the Focus Group discussion.

NUMBER AND COMPOSITION OF GROUPS

The number and composition of the focus groups will depend upon the project objectives as well as project time-frame and budget. Four groups is typical for a project but more or less are possible, although very large numbers of groups are uncommon. It is advisable to duplicate the composition of your most important groups.

RECRUITING OF PARTICIPANTS

Who does one get to go to the focus groups and how does one go about getting them to attend? Recruitment of participants takes place in a variety of ways. Market research companies often advertise, in newspapers for example, for individuals to assist in market research. The work takes about two hours for which the individual receives a cash payment of perhaps $20 or $25 (The amount will vary depending upon the composition of the group, such as teenagers or high-ranking executives). Interested individuals respond to the advertisement by telephone and are asked a few questions—screened for various characteristics—to see if they're eligible. If the individual meets the screening criteria, the time, date, and location for the focus group session is given. Usually the potential participant is telephoned a few days prior to the session to confirm attendance. At the end of the focus group session the participant receives a plain unmarked envelope containing the cash payment. Meanwhile, the name, phone number, and some information about this individual have been entered into a database of potentially agreeable participants of future focus groups; for this database is constantly growing. Companies may have restrictions on the number of times a person may attend sessions to avoid filling groups with "professional" focus group participants.

In my work in museum audience research, recruiting has taken place in a number of ways, but all potential participants are encouraged to take part by offering some sort of incentive. In keeping with the character of non-profit institutions cash payments are replaced by other incentives at little or no cost to the museum. These include free admission passes, invitations to exhibit openings, small souvenirs, posters, and catalogues. Free passes and other small gifts thank participants for their time, promote goodwill, and encourage repeat visits.

One effective way of recruiting group participants is through telephone lists supplied by the institution, such as membership lists and program registration lists. A second method is to recruit in-person and on-site at the museum for a focus group later that day. A third method is to recruit people at an alternative site such as a shopping mall. All of these methods will work. The one chosen depends upon the group composition that is required, such as local visitors, tourists, or non-users.

However, whichever method is chosen, the recruiting process should be closely supervised to avoid any unintentional bias.

Participants of focus groups are usually very pleased to take part in the sessions, and enjoy the opportunity to discuss the museum and to have input into future planning.

ROOM REQUIREMENTS

There are requirements for an effective focus group room. These include comfort, quiet, and set-up for discussion. Many market research companies have special focus group rooms which include two-way mirrors—so clients can watch and listen—audiotaping, and videotaping equipment. But you can prepare an appropriate room in your own institution as a focus group room and reduce project costs.

Refreshments should be nearby or available in the room. This too will facilitate a relaxed and comfortable discussion.

ANALYSIS AND REPORT

Sessions are usually audiotaped for purposes of analysis, but videotaping is also possibile. By reviewing the tapes the analyst organizes the discussion quotations, sentiments, and reactions by project objective, study guide question, and the issues which emerged from the groups.

Reports generally fall into two categories. First, there are the reports which present overviews of the results of the discussions with few or no direct quotations. Second, there are reports which present the results including the direct quotations from the proceedings. Know which one you are getting!

THE MODERATOR

The moderator is key to the success of the focus group method. Although there is a session study guide for the groups, it is a guide only. The concept of focus groups is to let the participants consider and speak in-depth about their reactions and what they feel are the issues. The moderator must draw out these issues and reactions, and, at the same time, follow the guide in such a way that it responds or relates to the expressed sentiments. Concerns of the moderator include:

Helping participants feel relaxed and comfortable.

Ensuring that everyone speaks, by preventing more talkative participants from monopolizing the group and encouraging quieter participants to speak.

Responding to issues and comments, but not answering questions which the participants are to answer or discuss.

Staying neutral and unbiased.

Keeping everyone on track and focused on the discussion topic.

Facilitating discussion among participants.

One of the most important concerns of the moderator is making sure that participants discuss what they themselves think and feel (such as reactions to a programming idea) and not what they think other people may feel (such as how the public may react). The moderator must explain that the museum wants participants to discuss their own attitudes and opinions rather than the perceived attitudes of others.

The moderator should always thank participants for their time and input, explaining that the results of the discussions will be used to develop and improve programs and services to the public.

The moderator must be trained in the skills of leading a focus group. Training includes: how to handle problem participants; how to encourage participants without putting words in their mouths; how to be sensitive to both the content/feelings of the participants statements and the objectives of the project; etc.

EXAMPLES FROM CASE STUDIES

Focus groups can yield useful information from users and non-users of museums, including:

Overall reactions, attitudes, expectations, image, and perceptions.

Reasons for visiting or not visiting.

Reactions to existing and proposed programs and services.

Needs and desires.

Likes and dislikes.

Sources of satisfaction and dissatisfaction.

Reasons for expressed attitudes.

Ideas for future programming and services.

Such inquiries can lead to a better understanding of an institution's audiences, including identification of an institution's existing and potential audience segments (for example, non-users, occasional users, and frequent users) and the psychographic profiles of these different audience groups. These studies can also identify planning issues, guidelines, and priorities for communications, programming, and visitor services. New ideas for the planning of future programs and services may also emerge in the discussions, as well as issues and criteria for future evaluation and research. While these studies may prove useful at any time, they are most effective at times of review and change, such as part of a strategic planning exercise, building renovation and expansion, or the planning of a new museum. The Manitoba Museum of Man and Nature in Winnipeg, for example, conducted focus groups with non-users in conjunction with other data collection activities—on site behavioral observations, surveys of visitors, and a community survey — as part of an institutional review and to assist in the development of a new marketing policy (Rubenstein & Barkow, 1986b). The Ontario Science Centre collected information from focus groups on tourists, local Toronto visitors, and non-visitors for general planning purposes (Rubenstein & Barkow, 1986c). Success with this project led to others, including one which focused on communications just prior to the hiring of a new advertising agency (Rubenstein, 1987a). This research resulted in a further identification of the different audience segments of the Ontario Science Centre, psychographic profiles of these audience segments, the issues that impact on visitation, attributes of an effective advertisement or promotion, and hypotheses of which audience groups would be most likely to attend the next major temporary exhibition. Overall these projects were not only useful, but were stimulating to planning efforts in general.

INFORMATION FOR SPECIFIC PROGRAMS AND SERVICES

Focus groups may be used effectively for information about specific programs and services. For example, feedback from representatives of potential audience groups of an upcoming exhibition can provide overall reactions and attitudes towards the concept of the exhibition, interest in attending or not attending and why, general background knowledge of the exhibition topic, any general misconceptions or confusions about the topic, and suggestions for specific displays. In this way focus groups are useful as a method of front-end evaluation in the early stages of planning. The National Museum of Science and technology in Ottawa recently used focus groups in this way. The information gleaned from the focus groups was followed-up by a survey for further specific and quantitative information on visitor baseline knowledge and interests (Rubenstein, 1988).

Focus groups can be a useful way to obtain information concerning services and programs other than exhibits in the early stages of planning. For example, the Ontario Science Centre conducted focus groups to assist in the development of a new membership program. Focus groups were held with potential audiences for membership. Study guide topics included: reactions to the concept of membership, reasons for membership, expectations, and desires for different membership benefits and categories (Rubenstein, 1986). When something new or different is proposed, focus groups can be a useful starting point for collecting information because the range of issues and reactions have not as yet been identified. Other examples of this use of focus groups include projects to identify issues and reactions to new applications of computers in museums (Rubenstein & Barkow, 1985; 1986a).

Once a new service or program is underway, focus groups can assist in fine-tuning and improvement. Such was the case in a project for continuing (adult) education at the Royal Ontario Museum in Toronto. Groups were held with program users and non-users towards the end of the two-year pilot period for this program. By that time the program was established, but there were a number of hypotheses concerning issues for further development and improvement. The research project tested these hypotheses and defined the issues. The project also showed that focus groups are useful for testing overall program objectives, and for identifying outcomes such as learning and motivation to join the museum. This is because the semi-structured format allows participants to discuss their own personal experiences, what they themselves get out of a program, and how this relates to their participation in the institution as a whole (Rubenstein, 1987b). The issues defined in the discussions also led to refinements of the regular program surveys.

Focus groups can provide psychographic information about audiences, reactions to institutions as a whole, and feedback to specific programs and services. Focus group projects can identify issues, guidelines, and priorities for planning, evaluation, and research. This qualitative form of research is particularly appropriate at times of review and change, when programs and products are new or embryonic, and the range of issues and reactions have not as yet been identified. The results gleaned from focus groups can also be used to develop an effective survey.

Rosalyn Rubenstein, M.M.St., CMC is principal of Rubenstein & Associates in Ottawa, a management consulting practice. A leading theorist and practitioner in the field, Ms. Rubenstein has consulted across Canada, in the U.S. and internationally. She can be reached at ruben@istar.ca

REFERENCES

Adams, G.D. *Museums' Public Relations.* Nashville: American Association for State and Local History, 1983. Higgenbotham, J. & Cox, K. (eds.) *Focus group interviews.*

Chicago: American Marketing Association, 1979.

Loomis, R.J. *Museum Visitor Evaluation.* Nashville: American Association for State and Local History, 1987.

Rubenstein, R. "Membership is a two-way street". *Reactions to the idea of Ontario Science Centre Management.* Toronto: Ontario Science Centre, 1986.

Rubenstein, R. "The Ontario Science Centre is the only place where you can get your hair to stand on end." *Audience issues and reactions for planning, promotion, and sport.* Toronto: Ontario Science Centre, 1987.

Rubenstein, R. "I came here to learn." *Reactions to the continuing education program at the Royal Ontario Museum.* Toronto: Royal Ontario Museum, 1987b.

Rubenstein, R. "Presentation is key". *Front-end evaluation study for 'Canada in Space'.* Ottawa: National Museum of Science and Technology, 1988.

Rubenstein, R. & Barkow, B. *Museum of Man public access to information systems, visitor perceptions of needs and prototype assessment study, activity one report.* Ottawa: Department of Communications, 1985.

Rubenstein, R. & Barkow, B. *Assessment National Museum of Man Telidon/Natal volunteer training project.* Ottawa: Department of Communications, 1986a.

Rubenstein, R. & Barkow, B. *Final report, public response and marketing strategy.* Manitoba Museum of Man and Nature, 1986b.

Rubenstein, R. & Barkow, B. "You have to experience it." *Focus groups and observations at the Ontario Science Centre.* Toronto: Ontario Science Centre, 1986b

Screven, C.G. Educational evaluation and research in museums and public exhibits: A bibliography. *Curator*, 27 (2), 147-165, 1984.

SETTING OFF ON THE RIGHT FOOT: FRONT-END EVALUATION

by Roger Miles and Clark Giles

Reprinted with permission of the authors. From *Environment and Behavior* 25 (6) November 1993, 698-709. 1993 by Sage Publications, Inc.

ABSTRACT: When exhibitions set out to impart information, they are a means of communication. Whether they succeed depends in large measure on the sensitivity of the designers to their audience, the visitors. Finding out what visitors are like is an aspect of evaluation, and the earlier this knowledge is fed into the design process, the greater the chance of success in producing good designs. Front-end evaluation gives insight into visitors and their requirements at the planning stage, when it can be used most effectively. The authors report on three projects where front-end evaluation has been used, one to plan a substantial series of exhibitions on the earth sciences, a second to design an exhibition on an important but unpopular group of animals, and a third to develop an exhibition for a specialist audience.

Some exhibits aim to do no more than display objects, without any explanation. Viewing the object is considered sufficient without any additional interpretive material to spoil the aesthetic effect. But most exhibition organizers have the intention of presenting information along with the objects they wish to display, perhaps something about the background or significance of the objects with other exhibitions, the main aim is to impart information. This means that most exhibitions are designed to be pieces of communication, and communication is a process that involves the active participation of two parties-both the transmitter of the information and the receiver. If this process is to be successful, the exhibition designer, when deciding how to transmit information, needs to understand the characteristics of the visitor as receiver. Visitors are not blank slates on which truth can be written; they have minds of their own and their own enthusiasms, prejudices, knowledge, and misconceptions, which all need to be taken into account. In designing exhibitions, there is an overwhelming need to understand visitors and to make sure that the exhibits speak to them in a language they can understand. Evaluation has a vital role to play in ensuring that this happens.

EVALUATION

Three different types of evaluation can be distinguished on the basis of when the work takes place. These are front-end evaluation before production of the exhibition, formative evaluation during production, and summative evaluation after production, when the exhibition is open to visitors (Miles, Alt, Gosling, Lewis, & Tout, 1988; Screven, 1990).

These three types of evaluation can also be distinguished on the grounds of what is evaluated. Thus front-end evaluation assesses the worth of plans before any money has been spent on developing them; formative evaluation assesses the success of mock-ups, normally using volunteers; and summative evaluation assesses the worth of finished exhibitions under real conditions.

In looking at these three types of evaluation in more detail, they will be treated here in reverse order (i.e., summative, formative, and front-end evaluation). This corresponds to the historical order in which the types of evaluation were adopted in exhibition work. It also corresponds to the direction in which emphasis has shifted over the last 10 years from summative to formative to front-end evaluation (Miles, 1988).

Summative evaluation is carried out with exhibits and real visitors during the course of normal visits. It uses a wide range of techniques to gather the data, it can use large samples, and it employs better statistical techniques than formative evaluation. However, summative evaluation is generally too late-the money has been spent, and there is none left to correct mistakes. It is also threatening to those whose work is evaluated, and, unless sensitively handled, can damage their self-esteem. The value of the evaluation may be undermined by the political difficulty of admitting that mistakes have been made. Summative evaluation is not, therefore, the most valuable way of using scarce evaluation resources. The only exception is where the evaluation is expected to give results of general value across a variety of exhibitions and museums, or when the results can be used to revise the exhibition or assist work on the next one. In the last case, the evaluation has the same value as front-end evaluation.

Formative evaluation is ideally quick and inexpensive. It is used to assess the potential of designs to communicate clear messages and should be carried out by the team designing the exhibits so that the threat felt when outsiders report on their work is eliminated. It gives the team some insight into what they need to do to improve the quality of the designs. Nevertheless, formative evaluation requires additional time and money which may not be readily available, and it gives incomplete information about how well the exhibits will attract and communicate with visitors under real conditions in the finished exhibition. As with much evaluation work, it cannot tell the design team how to correct the faults it has uncovered, and it may be inappropriate where exhibits (e.g., multiscreen audiovisuals) are difficult to mock up. Despite these problems, formative evaluation has an important role to play in exhibition development. However, it is a mistake to think that it is the most important method of evaluation. Indeed, if we acknowledge that visitors have an active role to play in the process of communication, we see that formative evaluation is most likely to succeed where the visitors are already well understood. This is the task of front-end evaluation. Front-end evaluation (Hayward & Loomis, in press; Miles et al., 1988; Shettel, 1992) sets out to answer a question: How well will the exhibition we are proposing to build work for the target audience? To answer this question, a range of information is collected, including:

- the audience's existing knowledge of the subject
- the audience's misunderstanding of the subject
- the audience's expectation of the exhibition and whether they will visit it
- the acceptability and intelligibility of the story line
- the appeal of the proposed treatment, including the media of communication

These data can come from specific sources, that is, from studies carried out especially to assist the planning of a particular exhibition, or from general sources, including visitor surveys at the museum in question, wider surveys (e.g., of the museumgoing habits or educational attainments), and research into visitor behavior. How can evaluation help in planning communication? The main tasks in planning an exhibition as a piece of communication are:

- to decide the aims, i.e., what is to be achieved
- to define the audience
- to decide the intellectual structure or story line, i.e., what is to be communicated, where to begin, and how to continue
- to choose the medium of communication to carry the messages to the audience

Front-end evaluation has a major role to play in each of these tasks. Formative evaluation in the literal sense of giving form to the communication has a role in deciding the structure and deployment of media when this involves the exact use of objects, words, and pictures, but it is of limited value in choosing media of communication or in defining the aims of, and audience for, an exhibition. The experience of interacting with visitors during formative evaluation may, however, cause the design team to reconsider the aims of the exhibition and the target audience.

Defining the target audience for an exhibition is an executive rather than an empirical task, though empirical data are involved. It is necessary to define a target audience because the range of people who might visit a museum, or who actually do, is heterogeneous, and an exhibition designed to please everybody would probably please nobody. The target audience chosen is likely to be a subset of the actual audience, which means that it must be defined in a way that is consistent with empirical knowledge of the actual audience.

Major problems arise in museums where there is little or no overlap between the target and actual audiences. This can happen, for example, if an expert curator who has no empathy with visitors is in charge of the exhibitions. A major role of front-end evaluation is to ensure that the target audience for an exhibition is defined in a way that is consistent with the actual audience. In fulfilling this role, front-end evaluation draws on general rather than project-specific sources of data.

THREE CASE STUDIES

THE GEOLOGICAL MUSEUM, LONDON

When the Geological Museum in London merged with the Natural History Museum in 1988, we found that the exhibitions were attracting only a small number of visitors, and these tended to be specialists rather than members of the general public. Front-end evaluation was therefore carried out to help develop new communications strategies by finding out

- what people understand by the term geology and which parts of the subject are of most interest
- reactions to nine ideas for new exhibitions
- the attractiveness of different types of display, that is , different media of communication.

Some 219 interviews were conducted with visitors to the Geological, Natural History, and Science museums, along with five group interviews (focus groups) covering all types of visitors to the three museums. The two approaches gave similar results. Thus visitors leaving the three museums were asked whether they felt the displays were aimed at the specialist or the general public.

The Geological Museum was seen as a museum for the specialist, and geology was seen as a dead subject, having little relevance to modern life, and as academic and boring. Some topics thought to be highly relevant to the study of geology (e.g., types of rocks) had low interest for visitors. On the other hand, some topics which had high interest for visitors (e.g., natural disasters) were thought to have low relevance to geology. Fortunately, a third group of topics was seen as both interesting and relevant to geology (e.g., North Sea oil, meteorites, and natural resources). These indicated how the museum might be arranged to attract more visitors and to succeed better at helping the public to understand earth science.

The appeal of different geological topics was explored in more detail by getting subjects to rank nine titles for possible exhibitions, with the following results:

1. The way the Earth works
2. The world of the past
3. What the Earth is made of
4. Geology made useful
5. Geology under London
6. Earth, water, air, and space
7. Regional geology
8. Earth for beginners
9. Seaside rock

When the proposed contents of these exhibitions were explained in more detail, some (3 and 7) lost part of their appeal but others (5, 6, and 8) gained.

The responses of subjects to five styles of exhibits (i.e., the different uses of media), in relation to these proposed exhibitions, were also recorded. The five styles were

- traditional: showcases with many objects and labels
- art gallery: few, beautiful objects and short labels
- static: objects, graphics, and a lot of text
- participatory: hands-on exhibits
- high-tech: large-scale, walk-around with videos or computers

The results showed that participatory and high-tech exhibits were always preferred over traditional and art gallery methods. However, for two of the proposed exhibitions (the world of the past and regional geology), static displays were preferred, because in these instances they appeared to be more appropriate.

This front-end evaluation gave rise to a number of recommendations which formed the basis of plans to redevelop the museum:

- Exhibition titles should convey "relevance to the visitor," not "relevance to geology"
- Geology should be portrayed as a dynamic, contemporary subject that affects all of our lives.
- The exhibitions should start with a simple introduction to applied geology on the ground floor of the museum.
- The upper floors can deal in more detail with pure geology. Participatory and high-tech exhibits should be used wherever possible, and visitors should be able to touch real objects.

ARTHROPODS

The second case study concerns the planning in 1982 of a large (550m2), new exhibition on arthropods (insects, spiders, crabs, and their relatives). Here, front-end evaluation involved two studies:

1. summative evaluation of an existing Insect Gallery
2. a survey of visitors" knowledge of, and feelings about, arthropods.

The summative evaluation study included interviews with 86 visitors (each interviewed before and after their visit) and unobtrusive observation of the behavior of another 75 visitors in the gallery. The aims were to discover who visited the gallery and what interests were. It turned out that the visitors fell into two groups, the specialists (27%) and general visitors (73%). The specialists were relatively more numerous in this gallery than in other exhibitions in the museum, because general visitors were only "fairly interested" in insects, which they saw as unpleasant pests and carriers of disease, therefore avoiding the gallery.

Subjects were asked to rank the topics in the exhibition prior to their visit for their intrinsic interest. Habitats and adaptation were clearly the most interesting and classification the least, with a group of topics in the middle of approximately equal appeal.

1. Habitats and adaptations
2. a. What makes an insect an insect?
   b. Insect biology
   c. Social instincts
   d. Insects as pests
3. Classification of insects

The effect of a visit on the middle group of topics was to make "what makes an insect an insect?" seem less interesting, and "social insects" more interesting. This showed that the treatment of the topic could make a difference to visitors' attitudes. One seemingly paradoxical result of asking visitors what they would like from the exhibition was the request by 33% of the sample, in an exhibition full of facts, for more information. This was evidently a plea for information that was relevant and accessible to general visitors as distinct from entomologists.

The two main recommendations that came out of this study were to present insects

in a more favorable light

in a way that enables visitors to make connections, that is by dealing with habitats and the importance of insects to humankind, rather than with the classification of insect groups.

The second part of front-end evaluation involved a survey of visitors' attitudes and knowledge about arthropods. It included 69 interviews with visitors arriving at the museum, and 76 with visitors leaving. To investigate people's feelings about arthropods, the subjects were first asked what they thought when they heard someone talking about the different groups. The results were:

insects: unpleasant thoughts; pests or spiders; otherwise, a wide range of comments

millipedes and centipedes: unpleasant creatures with lots of legs that crawl close to the ground and are found under stones

crabs: food and the seaside

spiders: unpleasant creatures that build webs, tend to be hairy with long legs.

As in the case of the Insect Gallery study, we found that visitors generally had a negative view of the group of animals in question.

Subjects tended to have some knowledge about the exoskeleton and parts of the body in arthropods, about the great number of insects in relation to other species, and about the life-cycle of the butterfly. However, they had little or no knowledge of what arthropods eat, their range of sizes, their molting and growth, or their freshwater habitats.

When asked their preference, only 3% of subjects wanted an exhibition based on the classification of arthropods, while 92% wanted one based upon natural history, principally because this would be more interesting, easier to understand, and better looking.

As a result of these studies, a new exhibition of arthropods was built and opened in 1989. It is based on the natural history of these animals, rather than on their classification, and it stresses the importance of arthropods to mankind. The exhibition has proved to be immensely popular with our visitors, in marked contrast to the old Insect Gallery.

BRITISH NATURAL HISTORY

The third case study concerns an exhibition designed for a more specialized target audience, committed amateur naturalists. As a matter of policy, the Natural History Museum decided that it should develop one gallery, not for the general visiting public, but for people who had a practical and long-lasting involvement with field studies. The idea was that such people, especially the younger ones, are significant in the biological community in Britain, and we should be doing something positive to support and encourage their commitment to natural history.

We had little experience of designing exhibitions for such visitors and therefore carried out front-end evaluation to discover what committed amateur naturalists would appreciate in a gallery and how best to organize it. Because the target audience for the gallery was likely to be numerically small, we decided to approach the evaluation through a few in-depth interviews designed to elicit qualitative information rather than by a large number of short questionnaires. Our first task was to define the characteristics of the target audience so we would be able to identify them among visitors at large. A series of five statements was drawn up to indicate a visitor's degree of commitment. Respondents agreeing that at least two of these described themselves were regarded as falling into the target audience.

- I belong to a natural history or some other equivalent society, club, and so on.
- I try to get out into the country at least once a month to pursue my interest in natural history.
- I own some equipment necessary to pursue my interest in natural history (e.g., binoculars, microscope, etc.).
- I read at least three books a year on natural history subjects.
- I regularly read magazines and newspapers on natural history subjects.

After screening a substantial number of visitors to the museum, 14 were identified as being "committed amateur naturalists" in these terms, and they took part in extended interviews.

The interviews concentrated on finding out potential visitors' views in one general and two more specific areas and what their expectations and requirements of such a gallery would be. We were keen to know whether it would be more useful for the fundamental organization of the gallery to be habitat by habitat, or whether a taxonomic arrangement (all the butterflies in one place, all the plants in another, for example) would be better. In addition, we asked which reference books the naturalists used habitually so that we could judge what kind of depth of information they found helpful.

As a result of this exercise, a series of recommendations was compiled which reflected the consensus view of the target audience and could be used in a practical way to plan the exhibition. The most important recommendations were as follows:

- The specimens in the gallery should be arranged by habitat rather than by classification.
- The exhibition should aim to cover as wide a range of groups as possible rather than the largest number of specimens.
- A variety of methods of presentation would be appreciated.
- Conservation should be an important theme to the exhibition.
- Urban habitats should be included along with wild ones.

The new exhibition was opened in 1983. Its organization followed the recommendations prompted by the evaluation, especially at the fundamental level, where it was divided into a series of habitat areas. A year after the opening, a summative evaluation project was carried out in the gallery. This confirmed that British Natural History was successful in attracting members of the target audience, who responded favorably to its design. In addition, several aspects of the gallery's contents were better understood by visitors who had visited the exhibition, notably the scientific background to nature conservation. The gallery had proved a worthwhile addition to what the museum had to offer amateur naturalists.

These three case studies show how front-end evaluation can be used to decide on communication strategies-in particular aims, structure, and media-for an entire museum or for individual exhibitions. They justify the conclusion that the earlier evaluation is carried out in the planning process, the better, both for the resources and quality of the final product.

Roger Miles is Head of the Department of Public Services at the Natural History Museum in London, where he has been responsible, over the past 17 years, for mounting a series of major new permanent exhibitions.

Giles Clarke is Head of Exhibition Planning and Education at the Natural History Museum in London. He joined the museum in 1973 and has been developing new exhibits since 1980.

REFERENCES

Hayward, J., & Loomis, R. J. Looking back at front-end studies. In D. Thompson, A. Benefield, S. Bitgood, H. Shettel, & R. Williams (Eds.), *Visitor studies: Theory, Research, and Practice* (Vol. 5) Jacksonville, AL: Center for Social Design.

Miles, R. S. Exhibit evaluation in the British Museum (Natural History). *ILVS Review: A Journal of Visitor Behavior*,1 (1), 24-33, 1988.

Miles, R. S., Alt, M. B., Gosling, D. C., Lewis, B. N., & Tout, A. F. *The design of educational exhibits* (2nd ed.). London: Unwin Hyman, 1988.

Screven, C. G. Uses of evaluation before, during and after exhibit design. *ILVS Review: A Journal of Visitor Behavior*, 1(2), 36-66, 1990

Shettel, H. Front-end evaluation: Another useful tool. *ILVS Review: A Journal of Visitor Behavior*, 2(2), 275-280, 1992.

CHAPTER 4

Theory

Formative Evaluation: Does Your Exhibition Attract and Hold Visitors' Attention? Do Visitors Know How to Use Your interactives? Do Visitors Understand Your Messages?

WHAT IS FORMATIVE EVALUATION?

Chandler Screven

Originally appeared in *Museum Visitor Studies in the 90's*, ed. by Sandra Bicknell and Graham Farmelo, London: Science Museum, 1993; also published in slightly different form in *Visitor Studies: Theory, Research, and Practice,* ed. by Don Thompson, Steven Bitgood, Arlene Benefield, Harris Shettel, and Ridgeley Williams, Jacksonville, AL: Visitor Studies Association, © 1993.

Will visitors understand what this exhibit is all about? Will visitors use this interactive device in the way we intended? In short—will the exhibit "work?"

These questions can be answered before the exhibit is complete and open to the public. Through formative evaluation, a dialogue with the audience is initiated at the outset of the development process that continues as the exhibition is planned, designed, and fabricated. This dialogue provides the information necessary to work toward the goal of creating exhibitions with the maximum level of educational effectiveness, the maximum emotional impact, and a minimum of mechanical and communication shortcomings. In short, formative evaluation leads to exhibitions that work better.

Formative evaluation can help reveal the needs and expectations of visitors and link them with the educational goals of museum professionals. Focusing on visitor needs does not mean pandering to visitors by presenting superficial interpretations of exhibit content. Finding out what our visitors know and what they get out of the exhibits we present may modify our views and priorities about an exhibit's messages and delivery methods. But the museum staff makes the final decisions about an exhibit's message, style of delivery, and content.

Formative evaluation is used most often during early phases of exhibit design, but many of the same techniques can be productively applied to exhibitions that are open to the public, including so-called permanent halls. In fact, formative methods are useful at any phase, including the upgrading of changeable components in installed exhibits.

Handmade mock-ups used during early design phases usually provide a reliable basis for predicting how the public will react to full-scale exhibitions. Research (see Griggs and Manning in the bibliography) suggests that although mock-ups are often crude, they can provide reliable visitor feedback. Formative evaluation can be used to successfully assess both effectiveness in communication (Do exhibit components get key messages across?) and the impact of delivery methods (How many visitors use prospective displays the way designers intended?) while the exhibit is unfinished aesthetically.

Mock-ups range from paper-and-felt-marker labels to full-sized prototypes of mechanical devices. The time it takes to produce mock-ups depends on the complexity of the exhibit's delivery system and how "mockable" they are. The evaluator may choose to explain and demonstrate particular exhibit concepts instead of actually fabricating the entire device.

You don't have to test everything. It is not necessary or practical to prototype every component of an exhibition, although this certainly can be done. The Science Museum of Virginia in Richmond, Natural History Museum in London, The Children's Museum of Indianapolis, and The Franklin Institute Science Museum in Philadelphia are among the museums that have made prototypes of every component of an exhibition on occasion. More typically, only a few critical, controversial, complex, or difficult modules are prototyped.

Formative evaluation is useful for examining the teaching efficiency of mock-ups, and can also yield information about the behavioral or motivational impact an exhibit might have on visitors.

Early formative testing can focus not only on cued testing of the teaching/learning efficiency of mock-ups but also on uncued (unobtrusive) observations of visitors' attention, time spent, level of involvement, and other affective behaviors.

Formative evaluation is often "quick and dirty"-lacking control groups, statistical analyses, and other rigid scientific procedures. It is usually conducted with a fraction of the funds, human resources, and time that controlled research requires. However, the process can be highly useful even if it is brief, narrowly focused, and based on a small sample. An hour of observing 10 visitors examining the instructions on a mock-up can provide a wealth of feedback.

While formative evaluation may lack the rigor of research, it is much more than simple trial and error; there's method behind it. There are many basic methods for "quick and dirty" studies that produce reliable data. The characteristics of good formative evaluation methods include: question clarification; systematic data collection on a small sample of visitors; and analysis of the data for decision-making purposes. To select the questions to ask, and to make use of the answers, evaluators use a theory or a model (several are offered in this book), rather than asking questions at random. The key word here is systematic. It is not just one observer's anecdotes or opinions formed after casually observing a few visitors.

Formative evaluation need not be conducted by professional evaluators and psychologists. Much evaluation can be effectively conducted by in-house staff without extensive training. Day-to-day formative evaluation is often best carried out by in-house teams, initially trained by experts and with periodic expert help. Staff background in human behavior, learning, and instructional design can be very helpful; museum administrators need to consider such requirements when hiring program development staff.

Designing educational exhibits assumes a general understanding of human behavior and informal learning in public areas. This knowledge allows reasonably well-educated guesses about what may or may not work. Formative evaluation fine tunes these assumptions, theories, and guesses, and reduces the likelihood of errors arising from the many unknown, unpredictable influences operating in open exhibit environments.

A basic premise of formative evaluation is that it is important to listen to visitors; to incorporate visitors' viewpoints into exhibitions. Formative evaluation is based on real visitor capabilities and limitations, not hypothetical audiences.

People undertaking formative evaluation should be curious and eager to find out about their audience-and they must be willing to admit that they don't know everything.

Formative evaluation can help exhibition development teams avoid arguments when team members disagree. The evaluator can bring empirical evidence to help sort out opinions. This evidence can relate to seemingly minor decisions, like the size of a knob, or to such major issues as whether or not to include a particular topic. Data are more convincing than an arbitrary opinion of a strong-willed member of the exhibit development team. Evaluation informs everyone; it tests everyone's ideas and opinions.

The team's job is to clarify the purposes and rationales of their exhibits, and then identify potential problem areas, develop clear questions to gather data, and use visitor feedback for problem resolution. Frequently, the evaluation process turns up wonderful discoveries. It may reveal additional content that needs to be included in the exhibition for full comprehension. And, it may reveal an unintended use of a manipulative device that adds an unexpected, yet valid dimension to the exhibition. These are some of the surprises that await the formative evaluator.

Chandler Screven's university teaching and research at the University of Wisconsin-Milwaukee centered on motivation, learning theory, attention, measurement, and instructional design. After 1980, scholarly activities mainly reflected work in informal settings in which behavioral research was applied to the systemaic study of visitors in informal settings like museums and how exhibit content, design, and other features in these settings influenced visitor motivation, knowledge, attitude, and understanding. Screven's contributions are associated with over 50 publications, international forums and symposia, and numerous on-site workshops worldwide. He is currently Principal of Screven & Associates located in Chicago.

Case Study

FORMATIVE EVALUATION OF EXHIBITS AT THE BRITISH MUSEUM

by Steven Griggs

Reprinted with permission of *Curator*, volume 12 (3). © The American Museum of Natural History, (1981): 189-201.

INTRODUCTION

How can an exhibition designer be fairly confident that his proposed exhibits will be successful? Until fairly recently such a question would only have been asked by a small minority, since most exhibition developers have believed, rather arrogantly, that they knew best and that whatever they came up with was bound to succeed. Failure, if admitted, was the fault of the visitor. This attitude is perhaps best expressed in the writings of Gunther (1880), one of the early Keepers of Zoology at the British Museum (Natural History).

"The exhibition will probably be found more liberal than may be deemed necessary by some of my fellow-labourers; but if a visitor should, on leaving the galleries, take nothing with him but sore feet, a bad headache, and a general idea that the animal kingdom is a mighty maze without plan, I should be inclined to believe that this state of bodily and mental prostration is the visitor's and not the curator's fault."

Fortunately, this state of affairs has been changing slowly over the last few years, and more museums are beginning to appreciate that the process of developing exhibitions should be accomplished less by decree and more by trying out and modifying ideas. This process of appraisal is usually termed evaluation.

We can make a useful distinction between "summative" and "formative" evaluation in museums (Screven 1976). Summative evaluation takes place with exhibits that are already installed in a gallery. Its aim is to provide information concerning how well the installed exhibits are functioning. Formative evaluation is somewhat different. It is carried out as an integral part of the development process, i.e., while exhibits are being developed, before they have been permanently installed. The primary aim of this form of evaluation is to test ideas for exhibits, and where these do poorly, to modify the design to correct its failings.

The New Exhibition Scheme at the British Museum (Natural History) considers evaluation to be an integral part of exhibition development (Clarke and Miles, 1980; Miles 1981; Miles and Alt 1979; Miles and Tout 1978). This article considers some of the methodological aspects of formative exhibit evaluation as it takes place at the BM(NH), as well as describing the process itself in two recent studies.

THE LITERATURE

Coming as I did from a background in psychology to work as an exhibition evaluator, one of my first moves was to turn to the relevant literature on museum evaluation. With a few notable exceptions the majority of published articles proved to be disappointing. There were too many anecdotal accounts and too few studies with rigorous scientific description. Where a more experimental approach had been adopted, the designs and procedures were often inadequate in answering the questions that had been posed.

While these comments should not be taken as a condemnation of the work that has been reported (indeed, I would rather such papers were written than nothing at all), the point I wish to make is that if we are ever to advance the process of evaluation in a museum setting we must begin to develop a meaningful literature.

METHODOLOGY

What are the main methodological considerations underlying evaluation? While summative and formative evaluation are complementary, there are certain fundamental differences between them in the way they are carried out at the BM(NH).

Summative evaluation is performed on the exhibits themselves in situ, and aims to provide information concerning how well these exhibits are functioning. This information may be collected in three ways: large-scale sample surveys of museum visitors; studies of the behavior of visitors; and educational evaluation of exhibits using pen-and-paper tests of knowledge (Alt and Morris, 1979). Summative evaluation is important for two reasons. First, it tells us how successful an exhibition is and whether all or parts of it need to be revised. Second, it provides more general information concerning the interaction of exhibits and visitors, and provides valuable results for future exhibition development as well as the construction and testing of theories of exhibit-visitor interaction. Summative evaluation is thus like any other form of research that relies upon the social sciences research model.

Formative evaluation, on the other hand, is carried out during development of the exhibit. The evaluation is based upon the storyline and objectives set out at an earlier stage. Formative evaluation is carried out not on the exhibits themselves, but on mock-ups of the exhibits. These often take the form of a poster displaying the text and graphics in a rough form. More elaborate mock-ups are required for interactive devices (See, for example, Eason and Linn, 1976).

The main goal of formative evaluation is to assess how well a particular set of mocked-up exhibits communicates its intended message to a particular group of visitors. However, this emphasis on the intended message or story line does not mean that other information is ignored. Formative evaluation, in one sense, starts as soon as an exhibition developer begins to reject one possible idea in favor of another. We can also use visitors' spontaneous comments to judge likes and dislikes. At a more formal level, we can investigate whether analogies are correctly interpreted, if text is readable, if colors are effective, and so on. This information can be acquired by using two basic techniques: interviewing small samples of visitors, and carrying out pen-and-paper tests. Observations of visitor behavior are usually not included because the visitors have been selected to take part, and this in itself may affect their response.

Another important consideration concerning the methodology is that it should reflect the aims and rationale of formative evaluation: we are not "hypothesis-testing" in the usual sense, nor are we attempting to generalize our findings to a larger group of either exhibits or visitors one of the aims of summative evaluation. Instead, we want to obtain information about specific mocked-up exhibits in order to make any necessary modifications, and, ultimately, to produce a set of successful mock-ups that can then be blue-prints for finalized exhibits.

The most appropriate models to adopt are not necessarily the social sciences laboratory model, in which all variables except one are controlled, or the statistical-inference model, by which one generalizes from random samples to larger populations. (For a more detailed discussion of the limitations of these approaches, see Levine, 1974 and Stoodley, 1980). Other models have an equally important role to play, including the criteria-reference approach, in which one examines what percentage of a sample has achieved a certain percentage mark in a test (see Popham, 1975). Yet another way of tackling the problem is to approach it from more than one angle. Instead of only using levels of statistical significance as the means of corroborating one's results, one looks for similar patterns in the results of several different approaches. For example, if an interview, a multiple-choice test, and a questionnaire all indicate that a particular piece of information is poorly communicated, we can fairly confidently conclude that the mock-ups have failed at this point.

This leads to another point about formative evaluation: while it can tell us if a mock-up fails, and sometimes why it is failing, it cannot, except in very general terms, tell us what would succeed in its place. The mock-up must be modified to take these failings into account, and then a second evaluation carried out, and, if necessary, a third and a fourth-an infinite regress!

In practice, the first evaluation will probably achieve one of two ends. In one case, where the mock-ups are judged to be largely successful, the evaluation will eliminate the majority of flaws and will result in a good approximation to some "ideal form." In this case, further evaluation would provide little more in the way of useful information.

In the second case, the mock-ups may require extensive, if not total, re-design. When this is the result, it becomes necessary to decide whether to try and rescue something from the existing mock-ups or to begin the whole development process from scratch. In either case, further evaluation is essential.

This, then, is a brief outline of formative evaluation as it is envisaged at BM(NH). It differs considerably in its methods from summative evaluation. Ultimately, however, the two are complementary since one aids in planning an exhibit, while the other tells us if the installed exhibit is successful.

TWO CASE STUDIES

The remainder of this article concentrates on the actual process of formative evaluation at the BM(NH). I shall draw upon two studies with which I have been involved.

The first of these concerned the Hall of Human Biology (Alt and Morris, 1979; Duggan, 1978, Miles and Tout, 1978). The first section of this exhibition, entitled "Living Cells," was revised, and the revision included an evaluation study of the new exhibits in a mocked-up form (Figures 1 and 2). The second study was also a revision of an existing exhibition, the first part of the "Dinosaurs and Their Living Relatives" exhibition (Hamilton, 1979), which explains how animals, including dinosaurs, can be grouped together. While it is general Museum policy to modify and continually update existing exhibitions, the two revisions discussed here arose for other reasons. For both exhibitions, the Museum commissioned a report by an independent, outside observer. These two reports criticized certain aspects of the exhibitions and prompted the Museum to make a decision to change them. The revisions considered here represent steps to implement this change.

These two studies allowed a comparison between two categories of exhibits first discussed by Schaeffer and Patsuris (1958): "factual" and "conceptual" exhibits. The "Living Cells" assembly consists of mainly factual exhibits (for example, "This is what a cell looks like."). The first part of "Dinosaurs and Their Living Relatives" largely consists of conceptual exhibits (for example, several exhibits relied upon the visitor understanding the concept of "relationship by descent").

METHOD

Both evaluation studies comprised three parts. Initially, an informal preview of the mock-ups was presented to Museum staff. This was followed by two surveys of visitors during which they were asked to narrate their version of the story and fill in a questionnaire.

When the mock-ups had been constructed, they were set up in a room adjacent to the public galleries. Members of the Museum staff were invited to attend a preview of the mock-ups and write down their comments. These were then put to use in two ways. First, to correct inaccurate factual information or to modify some point where the majority stated that something was unclear (for example, replacing a photograph that 60% of staff said was unclear). Where such changes were required, most were incorporated prior to any visitor survey, time permitting. Second, the comments were used to identify potential problem areas for further consideration (for example, "Will visitors correctly interpret this analogy?" or, "Is this text too complex for most of our visitors?").

This staff preview was followed by a survey of visitors. For the "Living Cells" study, 30 visitors participated in both parts, story and questionnaire. Since this required about half an hour to complete per visitor, two samples of 30 visitors each were employed for the "Dinosaurs" study.

Visitors were approached by the interviewer on a random basis. When a visitor agreed to participate in the survey he was taken to the room housing the mock-ups and allowed to have a good look at them. He was then taken to one side, out of sight of the mock-ups. The interviewer explained that the mocked-up exhibits attempted to tell a story. The visitor was then asked to provide his version of the story. A tape recording was taken of what was said, and transcripts were drawn up.

The "Dinosaurs" mock-ups largely consisted of conceptual exhibits, the content of which was likely to be complex. Since visitors may have found it difficult to articulate what they had seen, we constructed a short multiple-choice test based upon our version of the story for the "Dinosaurs" mock-ups. Key words or phrases were replaced with three alternatives of which only one was correct. A pre-test was administered to a small sample of visitors (N = 20) beforehand. When visitors had finished giving their version of the story, they were given a copy of the multiple-choice test to complete.

The final measure employed in both studies was a questionnaire. This was administered to visitors while they were seated in full view of the exhibits. Although different in content, the two questionnaires were similar in structure for both studies. Each exhibit was considered in turn. Visitors were first asked to interpret each exhibit by explaining in their own words what they thought it was about. In the previous test, visitors were asked to recall what they had seen; now they simply had to interpret what they saw in front of them.

The questionnaire also asked visitors whether they found anything confusing about each exhibit. Their responses allowed us to identify text that was unclear and similar problems. Finally, the questionnaire presented a series of questions specific to each mock-up. These questions often arose from the preliminary staff survey and tackled specific problem areas. For example, visitors might be asked to interpret a particular analogy that the Museum staff had thought might be confusing.

Thus, the two evaluation studies involved multiple approaches that attempted to cover various aspects of the mocked-up exhibits.

RESULTS

The visitors' versions of the story were tape recorded and transcribed. The transcriptions were subjected to content analysis. Basically, this involves systematically noting down which parts of the storyline are mentioned by each visitor. Content analysis revealed that for the "Living Cells" study, the main topic areas were mentioned by the majority of visitors. A rather different picture emerged from the study of "Dinosaurs." The average percentage of the sample mentioning the main topic areas was less than 20 %.

One reason for the poor performance for "Dinosaurs" could have been the conceptual complexity of the subject matter. The results of this test again indicated that many of the mocked-up exhibits were failing to communicate their message. Although there was a small but statistically significant improvement in scores between the pre- and post-tests, observation of individual test items revealed a rather different interpretation: even where there was a statistically significant improvement on the post-test, the actual percentage of correct responses was still quite low. For example, an improvement from 30 % to 60 % correct would almost certainly be statistically significant, but it still leaves 40 % who get the wrong answer. This demonstrates the advantage of a criterion-referenced approach over the statistical-inference model.

The final measure employed was the questionnaire that was administered to visitors in front of the mock-ups. For each exhibit, visitors were first asked to explain in their own words what they thought it was about.

This exercise produced some surprising results. Certain mock-ups were interpreted by the majority of visitors to be saying something totally at odds with the intended message. For example, one of the mock-ups from "Living Cells" was intended to illustrate the structure of the two sex cells and how these structures are specially adapted to perform particular functions. Most people overlooked this and stated that the exhibit was supposed to illustrate the moment of fertilization. We concluded that this confusion arose for two reasons. First, the exhibit was poorly positioned. It was part of a series of exhibits, beginning with an introduction to the two types of sex cells and where they are produced through how the sperm cells enter the woman's body and journey to the ovum. The exhibit in question was placed at the end of this sequence rather than at the beginning, since the exhibition developers felt that one could only appreciate the structural adaptations once one knew the functions. However, the logical interpretation of the exhibit in this position was that given by most people: the moment of fertilization. This interpretation was reinforced by the graphics, which suggested that the two cells were indeed meeting. The problem was easily resolved by repositioning the exhibit and carrying out minor modifications to texts and graphics.

The questionnaire also contained questions designed to provide information concerning areas of confusion, portions of text which were difficult to read, and other details specific to particular mock-ups.

DISCUSSION AND CONCLUSIONS

The results of the two studies could not have been more different, and they reflect the two extreme cases outlined earlier.

The "Living Cells" mock-ups were found to be largely successful. For most of the exhibits, only minor changes were called for. The evaluation study seemed to have ironed out most of the flaws, and we decided that no further evaluation was necessary before constructing the final version of the exhibits. In sharp contrast, we found that the mock-ups for the first part of "Dinosaurs" would require extensive, if not total, redevelopment. There appeared to be two main causes of failure. To begin with, visitors were not provided with sufficient information about the aims of the exhibition, or where it would lead. They were being presented with information without being told why, nor was the relevance of this information made explicit.

The second reason relates to a presupposition of the exhibition developers about the level of prior knowledge of the target audience. This point came over most clearly concerning the concept of "relationship by descent." This concept was never really explained by any of the mock-ups because it was assumed that the majority of visitors would already be familiar with it. The evaluation procedure clearly indicated how wrong this assumption was. More than one visitor clearly stated that he could "not understand how one can have a relationship between something that flies and something that walks." Exhibition developers may benefit from going to their audiences even before producing mock-up exhibits that assume a certain level of knowledge.

The final outcome of the "Dinosaurs" evaluation was a decision to redevelop the exhibits from scratch, including writing a new storyline and a new set of objectives, rather than attempt to salvage something from the first set of mock-ups. This work is now in progress and, of course, will involve a second evaluation.

Another finding which arose from both studies quite independently has allowed us to draw a generalization for future exhibits: Never illustrate a general concept with a specific example; instead use either analogy or multiple examples. One exhibit in each study violated this maxim and on both occasions visitors overlooked the general concept and interpreted the exhibit as being an illustration of the specific example. This was true even when the visitors were sitting in front of the relevant mock-ups.

Such "positive" findings are fairly uncommon and the outcome of both of these studies was mainly "negative" information. In other words, they tell us what will not work rather than what will work. This is a reflection of the present state of the art of formative evaluation. We are still not really sure what kinds of questions can be addressed satisfactorily. In particular, we do not know how rough a mock-up can be and still provide meaningful results, nor do we know an effective way of mocking-up certain classes of exhibits, such as audio-visual material or computerized displays. Furthermore, we do not know for certain how the results obtained using mock-ups relate to the final versions of exhibits. This knowledge can only come about through trial and error, further research, and summative evaluation studies. And this knowledge can only be disseminated by developing a meaningful literature.

The results of these studies, especially those for "Dinosaurs," should not, however, be seen in a negative light. The outcome of such studies can only be beneficial if exhibition developers approach the evaluation with the correct attitude, namely, that it is an aid to producing good exhibits, rather than a means of criticizing their efforts. In both studies, the exhibition developers found it extremely useful to meet their audience and to receive feedback first-hand. Too often, exhibits are designed without any direct input from visitors.

In the long term we saved ourselves time, money , and frustration. For each study, two exhibition developers constructed the mock-ups, taking approximately 3-4 weeks. Most of this time was spent devising methods to mock-up interactive games and similar devices. This was followed by the evaluation procedure, which was carried out by the author and the two exhibition developers. Approximately two weeks were required to design the study and a further two weeks to complete it, including time spent interviewing visitors and analyzing results. Our savings can best be appreciated by considering what might have happened if the evaluation had to been carried out and the original "Dinosaur" exhibition had been constructed in the public galleries. To later discover that they were a failure would mean either resigning oneself to having a poor exhibition taking up valuable floor space, or committing much more time and money to rectify the faults. Only by carrying out some kind of formative evaluation can the exhibition developer be reasonably confident that his proposed exhibits will be successful.

REFERENCES

Alt, M. B. and R. G. M. Morris. "The Human Biology Exhibition at the Natural History Museum." *Bulletin of the British Psychological Society* 32: 273-278, 1979.

Clarke, G. C. S. and R. S. Miles. "The Natural History Museum and the Public." *Biologist* 27: 81-85, 1980.

Duggan, T. "The Shape of Things to Come? Reflections on a Visit to the Hall of Human Biology, South Kensington." *Museums Journal* 78: 5-6, 1978.

Eason, L. P. and M. C. Linn. "Evaluation of the Effectiveness of Participatory Exhibits." *Curator* 19: 45-62, 1976.

Gunther, A. C. L., "Address to the British Association." *Report of the Fiftieth Meeting of the British Association for the Advancement of Science,* London: J. Murray. 591-598, 1880.

Hamilton, W. R. "Heritage: Dinosaur Relationships." *New Scientist*, 81: 888-889, 1979.

Levine, M. "Scientific Method and the Adversary Model: Some Preliminary Thoughts." *American Psychologist* 29: 661-677, 1974.

Miles, R. S. "Information as an Experience: Exploitation of a Museum's Resources." Paper presented at the Aslib 115 LA Joint Conference 1980. London: *The Library Association*, 1981.

Miles, R. S., and M. B. Alt, "British Museum (Natural History): A New Approach to the Visiting Public." *Museums Journal* 78: 158-162, 1979.

Miles R. S. and A. F. Trout. "Human Biology and the New Exhibition Scheme in the British Museum (Natural History)." *Curator* 21: 36-50, 1978.

Popham, W. J. *Education Evaluation*. New York: Prentice Hall, 1975.

Schaeffer, B. and M. B. Patsuris. "Exhibits and Ideas." *Curator* 2: 25-33, 1958.

Screven, C. G. "Exhibit Evaluation-A Goal-Referenced Approach." *Curator* 19: 271-290, 1976.

Stoodley, K. D. C. "Statistical Inference in the Social Sciences." *Educational Research* 23: 51-56, 1980.

CHAPTER 5

Remedial Evaluation: How Do We Improve an Exhibition After Opening

THE CLASSIFICATION OF EXHIBIT EVALUATION: A RATIONALE FOR REMEDIAL EVALUATION

by Stephen Bitgood and Harris Shettel

Reprinted from *Visitor Behavior* 9 (1) Spring, 1994, 9 (1), (Spring 1994), 4-8. © Center for Social Design

It is said that Eskimos have over a dozen names for snow, no doubt reflecting their intense interest in, and "need to know" about, this important element of their environment. Most of us get by with one name, snow, although skiers talk about wet dry, powdery, base, etc. One might argue that we tend to develop a nomenclature that fits our particular needs. However, there is not always agreement on the assignment of names, especially when the thing or things being named are not tangible, discrete objects, but processes that occur over time.

The field of visitor studies is an interesting case in point, having evolved over the past 30 years or so into a professional discipline with a rather sizable body of literature and an international group of practitioners and clients. It would be surprising indeed if this rapid growth and development could occur without debate not only over what we do but what we call what we do.

Roger Miles (1993), in his presentation at a conference titled, Museum Visitor Studies in the 90s, held September 1993 in London, raised the naming issue very directly by challenging the need to introduce a fourth term, remedial, to our armamentarium, arguing that the three terms that have been well established over recent years (front-end, formative, and summative) are quite sufficient to account for all the various activities that fall under the general heading of exhibit evaluation. While not the major point of his presentation (which is an elegant, not-to-be-missed defense of the methodology and philosophy of evaluation), it is nevertheless an important issue that deserves further discussion.

A brief history of exhibit evaluation terminology should help bring the issue into perspective. Early evaluations tended to be what we now call summative, even though that term was not introduced until later. That is, the questions being asked were essentially some variation of "How successful was the completed exhibition?", often defined in terms of how many and what kinds of people came to see the exhibition, what they did in the exhibition, and sometimes what they liked and disliked about their experience. These evaluations were essentially seen as management tools that helped to determine whether doing the exhibit was worth the time and expense involved and whether or not similar exhibits were worth supporting in the future. Corporate and government entities tended to sponsor these early exhibit evaluation efforts.

In the early 1960s, the kinds of questions asked about exhibits shifted, with greater emphasis being given to a more diagnostic kind of analysis-"How do the various elements that go to make up an exhibit contribute to its effectiveness in terms of reaching clearly defined (affective and cognitive) visitor objectives?" While still "summative" in terms of when the data were collected, there was the added notion that a body of knowledge could be obtained that would lead to an applied science of exhibit effectiveness.

This increased sophistication in the analysis of the exhibit medium led to the notion that if one could obtain diagnostic information about exhibit effectiveness during the development of the exhibit, one could avoid mak-

SHETTEL'S (1968) CLASSIFICATION OF EVALUATION

Purpose of Evaluation		When It Is Carried Out		
		Before	During	After
	Improvement	—	Mock-up Validation	—
	Determining Success	—	—	[Summative]

Figure 1

ing costly "errors" that would show up in the finished product. This idea was not new, having been an integral part of the development cycle used by the military in the preparation of training materials. Early versions of films, lesson plans, programmed instruction books, display devices, etc., were routinely tested on members of the target audience and revised, based on clearly defined performance outcome measures. Some courses and supporting materials went through several iterations before they met a pre-established level of effectiveness.

When this idea was adapted and applied to the exhibit medium (Shettel, et al, 1968; Shettel, 1973) it was called mock-up validation, and was intended to be applied only during the development of the initial exhibit. In the Shettel, et al. (1968) study, the exhibit mock-up materials were used first to validate the idea that visitor responses to a mock-up would correlate adequately with their responses to the completed exhibition (which they did), and second, as a research vehicle to study the impact on visitors of variations in such things as label length and readability level, use of visuals, use of audio, etc. (This latter use of inexpensive mock-ups to do carefully controlled studies of exhibit variables is still underutilized.)

At this point in our history, the classification of exhibit evaluation could be shown in a simple two by three table (Figure 1 above). ("Summative" is placed in brackets to indicate that the term was applied only later in the history of visitor evaluation classification.)

In an independent development in the field of educational psychology, Michael Scriven (1967) proposed that the terms "formative" and "summative" be used to describe evaluation in formal educational settings. The term "formative" was used when attempting to improve the effectiveness of an educational program and "summative" to determine the value of a completed program (e.g., decide to continue or terminate). Scriven's terms are commonly used in formal education today. For example, in higher education, course evaluation instruments are often used as feedback to faculty for self-improvement (formative evaluation), and/or for making decisions about promotion and merit pay (summative evaluation).

Chan Screven (1976) saw the value of adopting these terms for the work being done in exhibit studies and articulated this notion in his seminal *Curator* article:

> "Formative evaluation takes place during planning and constructing an exhibit, or modifying a new one, and the results are used to change and improve elements of the exhibit to achieve its intended effects on visitor learning and performance. Summative evaluation takes place after an exhibit is installed, and the results establish its overall effectiveness with respect to the original goals. Summative evaluation provides the basis for deciding whether or not the exhibit, or its design features, should be continued, repeated, removed, and so on." (Screven, 1976; p. 274).

For purposes of comparison, we have placed the Scriven/Screven evaluation model into a two by three contingency table (Figure 2 page 71). It is immediately apparent that this model differs significantly from the Shettel at al. (1968) model, using the new term "formative" to include any effort carried out to change and/or improve elements of the exhibit whenever such work is done-before, during, or after even though the purpose of evaluation is different at each of these stages (e.g.,

SCREVEN'S (1976) CLASSIFICATION OF EVALUATION

Purpose of Evaluation	When It Is Carried Out: Before	During	After
Improvement	Formative	Formative	Formative
Determining Success	—	—	Summative

Figure 2

"before" and "during" are preventative, "after" is corrective). Summative evaluation, on the other hand, is shown in each model as occurring only after the exhibit is completed (when) and only to determine the overall success of the completed exhibit (purpose).

The potential for "muddle" had now been firmly established, and it created no end of confusion when one person used "formative" in the Shettel sense only to mean doing evaluations during actual exhibit development and another person used "formative" in the Screven sense to include making changes to a completed exhibit. "When" and "Why" were intertwined. One person's formative was another person's summative!

As the field of visitor studies matured, a third type of evaluation was identified: front-end evaluation. This notion came from what was originally called "front-end analysis," apparently first used by J. H. Harless (1970) to assess job performance deficiencies prior to developing training course material. The need for exhibit management teams to do careful front-end analyses was well recognized in exhibit development (see Miles, et al., 1982). But this front-end work should be more than careful budgeting and planning by experts. It should include the testing of exhibit ideas by collecting information from potential visitors about their pre-knowledge, misconceptions, attitudes, interests, etc. on the subject matter of the exhibit. Such information can then be used to refine or change the goals and objectives of the exhibit, helping to decide which educational messages should be emphasized, which omitted, etc. (This idea has roots in both the behavioral and cognitive sciences, where the importance of beginning any educational experience at a point where a meaningful connection can be made with previous experiences was recognized.)

Front-end evaluation presented both semantic and practical problems to the existing evaluation models. Should it be subsumed under the formative evaluation concept because it helps to modify and (presumably) improve the exhibit (la Screven, 1976), or should it be given its own identity and thus make the 1976 model obsolete? Confronted with this dilemma, Screven (1986) at first described front-end analysis as the "pre-design stage" of a two-stage formative evaluation process. Later, Screven (1990) clearly made a distinction between front-end and formative evaluation and formative and summative evaluation. Finally, the muddle was eliminated (or at least greatly minimized). But, Screven was not content simply to modify his original scheme. He saw the need to carve out yet another kind of evaluation that he felt deserved a separate name.

What precipitated this development was the growing recognition that many installed exhibits, even those that enjoyed the benefits of front-end and in-process formative evaluations, were still "performing" at levels well below their potential. If visitor data were collected to identify and diagnose the precise nature of these problems, at least some of them could be corrected. A sensible notion, and one that had not escaped others, including Miles (1986). But, is this step distinctive and important enough to deserve its own name? Again, if the original Screven model were adhered to, such an activity would simply be another form of formative evaluation, even though it was carried out on the completed exhibit. On the other hand, if we allow "When" rather than "why" to be the controlling factor, such work would be considered to be a summative evaluation.

SCREVEN'S (1990) CLASSIFICATION OF EVALUATION

Purpose of Evaluation		When It Is Carried Out		
		Before	During	After
	Improvement	Front-end	Formative	Remedial
	Determining Success	—	—	Summative

Figure 3

After a good deal of soul searching and conversations with others in the field, Screven opted for giving this type of evaluation a separate identity and name, remedial evaluation. As shown in Figure 3 above, the original ambiguity between design stage and purpose of evaluation has now been addressed, with planning associated with front-end evaluation, preparation with formative evaluation, post-installation improvements with remedial evaluation, and overall assessment with summative evaluation.

In addition to eliminating the confusion of having formative evaluation at different development stages, there may be another good reason to make a distinction between formative and remedial evaluation, both of which attempt to improve exhibits. As Screven (1990) points out, a different set of variables (between-exhibits) is often present when evaluation occurs after the exhibit is installed. That is, problems such as circulation through the collection of exhibits in that area, distracting influences of other exhibit displays, etc. become very evident. During the design stage when mock-ups of exhibit elements are being tested in isolation, the problems tend to be within-exhibit, including such factors as the layout of a particular display, wording and placement of text, etc. (For a more detailed discussion, see Screven, 1990.)

Miles (1993), in his London paper, criticizes Screven's (1990) latest classification scheme, arguing that using this distinction (between- and within-exhibit factors) as a dimension for classifying evaluation types is not appropriate. In the words of Miles, it results in "a classification based on overlapping categories, leading to redundancy and the risk of muddle." However, Screven's classification is not based on the between/ within-exhibit difference; it is clearly anchored to the dimensions of when it occurs and its purpose, and therefore is not any more of an overlapping framework than Miles' own classification described below.

Miles' (1993) attempt to simplify the evaluation terminology may, in fact, have inadvertently increased the semantic confusion. He argues that Michael Scriven's distinction in terms of the purpose of evaluation is not useful to exhibit settings. Miles proposes we restrict ourselves to three types of visitor evaluation (front-end, formative, and summative) based on both when the evaluation is being carried out (before, during, or after design) and what is being evaluated (plans, mock-ups, or the completed exhibit). Figure 4 (page 73) illustrates Miles' classification model. As can be seen by comparing this model with Screven's (1990) model, the critical difference is whether evaluation types are classified by purpose or by what is being evaluated.

According to the Miles model, evaluation whose purpose is to improve exhibits can be called either summative or formative evaluation. Summative evaluation includes a period of six to twelve weeks of fine tuning after the exhibition is installed. Miles considers these post-installation improvements as part of the normal process of summative evaluation. However, if mock-ups are used after installation, he would consider this a return to the design phase and such work then becomes formative evaluation.

DIFFERENCES BETWEEN CLASSIFICATION SCHEMES

It is important to emphasize again that the differences between the Screven and Miles classification schemes are more semantic than procedural. Both schemes account for improvements at each stage of exhibit design. Nevertheless, four differences can be identified:

MILES' (1993) CLASSIFICATION OF EVALUATION

What is Being Evaluated / When it is Carried Out

	Before	During	After
Plans	Front-end	—	—
Mock-ups	—	Formative	—
Completed Exhibit	—	—	Summative

Figure 4

1. *Classification according to purpose or what is being evaluated.* The major difference between schemes is how one of the dimensions is being defined. Miles defines formative in terms of both the stage (during design) and what is evaluated (mock-ups). Mock-ups are used only during the design stage, but the design stage, by definition, occurs whenever mock-ups are being used (even to the improvement of a completed exhibit). When mock-ups are being tested on an exhibit that has already been completed and installed, the project, by definition, returns to the design stage.

Screven's scheme reduces the above confusion in terminology by defining evaluation type according to its stage and its purpose. Thus, formative evaluation takes place only in the preparation stage (during design) while remedial evaluation refers to improvements on completed exhibits (after design). The use of mock-ups in the post-installation stage is associated with remedial evaluation according to Screven's model. But, remedial evaluation can also include other attempts to improve a completed exhibit that do not involve the use of mock-ups (changing location of objects, changing layout, deleting elements of the exhibit, etc.).

Miles states that any evaluation that takes place after design (after installation) is normally summative evaluation; if mock-ups and new designs are involved, it is formative evaluation." This creates considerable confusion between pre-installation and post-installation evaluations that use mock-ups.

2. *Consistency with accepted usage.* Screven's classification based on the purpose of evaluation is consistent with the common distinction between formative and summative evaluation used in formal educational evaluation (e.g., Screven, 1967). Miles' scheme (based on what is being evaluated) is likely to confuse those familiar with the usage of evaluation terminology from the formal education literature.

3. *The role of the subject matter of evaluation.* Miles argues that Screven's definition of remedial evaluation is based on its subject matter ("between-exhibit problems rather than within-exhibit problems") and results in overlapping categories, leading to muddle. But, a careful reading of Screven (1990) will show that his concept of remedial evaluation is based on its purpose rather than on its subject matter-both between-exhibits and within-exhibit evaluations are grist for the remedial evaluation mill. However, even if the within-exhibit problems are minimized by front-end and formative evaluations, it is difficult to anticipate the between-exhibits problems that occur once the entire exhibition is placed on the floor.

4. *Amount of emphasis on improving completed exhibits.* While Miles (1988) has used evaluation for exhibit renewal at the Natural History Museum (London) for several major exhibitions, his writings suggest that he considers this type of evaluation more problematic than does Screven. Miles and Clarke (1993) state that evaluation after the exhibit is installed "is generally too late-the money has been spent, and there is none left to correct mistakes." Screven (1990), on the other hand, argues that a percentage of the total budget should be reserved for improvements after the exhibit is installed. This is a "bang for the buck" issue that needs more study. Cost-effectiveness analyses might shed light on this issue.

SUMMARY AND CONCLUSIONS

What's in a name? Maybe a rose by any other name would smell as sweet, but the fact is that we seem to need dozens of names for roses. Einstein said that things should be made as simple as possible, but not too simple. Miles claims his terminology is simple and straightforward-three stages and three kinds of evaluation. But this simplicity becomes illusory when one begins to dig deeper. The same activities change their position in the model depending on why they are carried out. Thus, summative becomes formative if you use mock-ups to make changes to the completed exhibit; after becomes during; post-occupancy becomes development. The Miles model does not map the reality of the various activities that can make a difference in the effectiveness of the finished product. Adding the term remedial to account for these kinds of post-installation improvements seems to us to avoid muddle, not contribute to it. It does add a new name to the list, but the term has the same kind of self-descriptive qualities that the terms front-end, formative, and summative have.

Use of the term remedial evaluation may encourage a change in current museum practice of leaving completed exhibits alone. As Miles suggests, there is the philosophy that once an exhibit is installed, it is finished-period. We hope that attention to the remedial process will encourage more museums to see the value of both renewing exhibits and incorporating the process of fine-tuning newly completed exhibits. There may be three arguments for remedial Evaluation: (1) It is cheaper than developing a new exhibit; (2) Renewal can incorporate the successful elements of an exhibit and eliminate unsuccessful ones; and (3) Renewal can incorporate the latest knowledge in the exhibit's subject area as well as the latest exhibit development techniques.

Stephen Bitgood is Professor of psychology at Jacksonville State University and President of the Center for Social Design. He is currently on the editorial boards for Environment and Behavior, Visitor Studies Today, and InterpEdge. He was the founder of the Visitor Studies Association and served as editor of Visitor Behavior and several volumes of Visitor Studies: Theory, Research, and Practice. In addition, he has published articles and chapters on various topics dealing with visitor research and evaluation.

Harris H. Shettel has been active in visitor-related museum studies for more than 30 years, with over 20 published papers and articles in the field and has presented professional papers and conducted symposia and workshops throughout the U.S., Canada, Europe, and Asia. Shettel received a graduate degree in industrial and organizational psychology from Wayne State University in 1952, and he is currently a museum evaluation consultant with an office in Rockville, MD.

REFERENCES

Harless, J. *An Ounce of Analysis (is worth a pound of objectives)*. McLean: VA: Guild Publications, 1970

Miles, R. Lessons in "Human Biology": Testing a Theory of Exhibition Design. *International Journal of Museum Management and Curatorship*, 5(5), 227-240, 1986.

Miles, R. Exhibit Evaluation in the British Museum (Natural History). *ILVS Review*, 1(1), 24-33, 1988.

Miles, R. Grasping the greased pig: Evaluation of Educational Exhibits. In S. Bicknell and Graham Farmelo (eds.), *Museum Visitor Studies in the 90s*. London: Science Museum of London. Pp. 24-33, 1993.

Miles, R., Alt, M., Gosling, D., Lewis, B., & Tout, A. The Design of Educational Exhibits. London: Allen & Unwin, 1982.

Miles R., & Clarke, G. Setting Off On the Right Foot: Front-End Evaluation. *Environment and Behavior*, 25(6), 698-709, 1993.

Screven, C. G. Exhibit Evaluation-A Goal-Referenced Approach. *Curator*, 19(4), 271-290, 1976.

Screven, C. G. Exhibitions and Information Centers: Principles and Approaches. *Curator*, 29(2), 109-137, 1986.

Screven, C. G. Uses of Evaluation Before, During, and After Exhibit Evaluation. *ILVS Review*, 1(2), 36-66, 1990.

Scriven, M. The Methodology of Evaluation. In R. E. Stake (ed.), Curriculum Evaluation. *American Educational Research Association Monograph Series on Evaluation*, No. 1. Chicago: Rand McNally, 1967.

Shettel, H. Exhibits: Art Form or Educational Medium? *Museum News*, 52, 32-41, 1973.

Shettel, H., Butcher, M., Cotton, T., Northrop, J., & Slough, D. Strategies for Determining Exhibit Effectiveness. Report No. AIR E95-4/68-FR. Washington, DC: American Institutes for Research, 1968.

Case Study

TEAM PRACTICE IN REMEDIAL EVALUATION: IMPROVING EXHIBITS THROUGH FORMATIVE EVALUATION

by David Taylor

© New York Hall of Science, 1991. Originally appeared in *Try It! Improving Exhibits through Formative Evaluation*, ed. by Samuel Taylor and Beverly Serrell (Washington, D.C.: Association of Science Technology Centers, and New York: New York Hall of Science, 1991)

A team had been assembled to work on a new traveling exhibit at the Pacific Science Center. The team was comprised of the designer, evaluator, several of the fabricators, and the content specialist for the exhibit. Some members of the team were new to the Science Center and most were new to the idea of prototyping and evaluation.

It was important that the members of the group function as a team and be able to prototype and evaluate the exhibit they would be developing. Patty McNamara from the Science Museum of Virginia came to lead the group through a practice session.

We chose an exhibit in whose development none of the team members had been closely involved, so that no one's feelings would be hurt when changes were suggested. We selected the Bicycle Gyro, a small exhibit in our Science Playground physical science exhibition. It was relatively simple with parts that could be easily reconfigured and instructions and interpretive copy that could be easily changed.

On the first day, the team gathered on the exhibit floor a short distance from the Bicycle Gyro, close enough so that we could still overhear visitors' comments. Within a few minutes, several problems became obvious to all of us. The instructions were facing in the correct direction for approaching visitors, who would read the first line of instructions and start doing the activity, which invited them to mount the platform. But once on the platform, visitors could no longer read the instructions. If the evaluator had been the only observer and had come back to report the problem to the other team members, they might have thought the problem trivial or that the evaluator was just finding fault and making more work for them. By seeing the problem firsthand, they became part of the process of finding the solution.

The instruction panel was moved and we continued to observe. The next step in the instructions told visitors to spin the bicycle wheel and then pick it up. This required them to bend over quite far, so we moved the wheel stand up onto a box where they could more easily reach it while on the platform. This helped, but we noticed visitors were still having problems keeping their balance while trying to spin the wheel and pick it up.

It appeared that we needed to change the order of the instructions. We instructed visitors to spin the wheel while standing on the floor, and then pick the wheel up before mounting the platform. We also used this opportunity to enlarge the lettering; some visitors were having a hard time reading the instructions because the type was too small. The revised instructions were done with felt marker on colored board-fast, easy, cheap, and easy to change again.

We noticed that most visitors found this a much easier sequence. We also noticed that several visitors played with the wheel after picking it up, but before mounting the platform. They tilted the wheel back and forth in the same way the instructions asked them to once they mounted the platform. These visitors seemed to start making observations about the forces on their arms, whereas those who mounted the platform first seemed to notice only that the forces made the platform go around. Thus, the visitors taught us a new way to use the exhibit, and we incorporated it into the instructions. This is an example of how visitors can unexpectedly teach us how to improve exhibits.

All of these activities and changes were completed in a matter of a few hours. If we had stopped there, we would already have had a better exhibit. We continued to observe and eventually interviewed some of the visitors who had finished using the exhibit. Several told us we should have smaller bicycle wheels for children. This sounded like a good idea, so a member of the group picked up a smaller wheel on his way home that night. By 10:00 am the next day we were ready to observe a school group using the new, smaller wheel.

The smaller wheel was the right size for children, but we found that no matter how fast they spun it, it just didn't have the momentum to cause the platform to move the way the bigger wheel did. We knew that one of the causes was the amount of mass at the outside of the wheel, so we added a length of heavy chain around the inside of the tire. Even with this addition, there still wasn't enough momentum.

Several of us knew the physics of angular momentum and the three primary variables: distance from the axis of rotation; the amount of mass; and the speed of rotation. But it wasn't until we went through prototyping that we really learned what these concepts mean in a kinesthetic (hands-on) experience. The smaller wheel just didn't work. Our solution was to tell younger visitors to pick up the larger spinning wheel from the side by only one of the handles. This worked for them, and it didn't interfere with the results when they mounted the platform.

We changed the following factors in less than a full work day:

the placement of the instructions
the order of the instructions
the size of the type
the arrangement of the exhibit elements
the size of the parts

The experiment with the smaller wheel was a failure, but the other changes helped make this a better exhibit. It was a valuable lesson for the team and a good way to learn that evaluation and prototyping can really improve the visitor's experience.

David Taylor is Director of Science for the Pacific Science Center. During twenty plus years with the Science Center, Mr. Taylor has developed more than 30 major exhibitions including Starlab, Computer Works, Body Works, Kid Works, Science Carnival, Whales Giants of the Deep, Tech Zone, Mostly Music and the Science Playground. David also oversees facilities operations and computer services for the Science Center's nine buildings site. Mr. Taylor has worked in the areas of computers, public radio and astronomy education prior to coming to the Pacific Science Center. He has degrees in Oriental Philosophy, Sociology and Computers and an MBA in organizational leadership.

CHAPTER 6

Summative Evaluation: Determining an Exhibit or Program's Effectiveness: What Works? What Doesn't? What Are You Doing Right?

THE RAIN FOREST IN MILWAUKEE: AN EVALUATION

by Mary S. Korenic
Allen M. Young, Curator of Zoology

Reprinted with permission of *Curator*, 34 (2), (1991), 144-160. © The American Association of Natural History, 1991.

"Rain Forest: Exploring Life on Earth" opened as the Museum's new Biology Hall in November 1998 after five years of research, planning, and production. Its mission is to communicate the themes of diversity, interrelationships, and commonality among living organisms.

It is set in the environment of an American tropical rain forest. The 11,000-square-foot gallery contains more than 70 cases featuring tropical specimens and educational information; 32 sound-effects speakers broadcasting the sounds of howler monkeys, birds, cicadas, and a tropical thunderstorm; five video theaters; and an elevated walkway through a simulated forest canopy. Informational exhibit text is presented on display backgrounds, on participatory flip panels, on pushbutton-activated "answer" panels, and "look-into" microscope eye pieces. Some forest-life sound effects are pushbutton-activated, and motion detectors initiate narrated informational programs. Ten video monitors feature both passive and interactive touch-screen programs. (See Curator 32/3: 229-44 for an in-depth description of the exhibit and planning process.) Topics covered in the hall include:

Natural Selection; Evidence for Evolution; Patterns of Evolution; The Struggle for Survival; Partnerships for Survival; Living Things and Their Environment; The Cell; Structuring Life; Classifying Living Things; Tropical Biomes; Layers of the Rain Forest; Dynamics of the Rain Forest; The Vanishing Rain Forest; Biological Diversity; Temperate vs. Tropical Forests; At the River's Edge; The Scientist in the Field, in the Museum, and in the Lab.

During the year preceding the opening, prototypes of 14 major exhibits were evaluated to determine whether their topics were understandable and whether interactive elements were effective. Still others were at a stage where, if changes were indicated, implementation was possible. More than 150 randomly-selected visitors were interviewed; and their responses to a set of questions were evaluated by a team that included curators, an educator, the script writer, and exhibit designers. When this formative evaluation revealed that visitors were not getting the message, changes in label text and/or design and even more substantive changes were made-and the exhibits were then retested.

The new exhibit received considerable publicity-both locally and nationally-and special recognition at the AAM Curators' Committee Exhibit Competition. Over 60,000 persons visited the hall during the first six weeks after the opening.

The National Science Foundation, which contributed substantially to the exhibit, additionally funded a summative evaluation, to be conducted by the Museum in the year following the opening. In 1990, the full report was published and is available from the Museum. This paper is drawn from that report. The goals were (1) to evaluate the exhibit's effectiveness in getting its message across, (2) to provide information that could be used to alter and modify exhibits where desirable, and (3) to provide a guide for future exhibit planning. Two studies were made, one of visitor behavior and the other of visitor responses to questions.

GOAL 1: DETERMINING EXHIBIT EFFECTIVENESS

In January 1989, measuring instruments were designed and pilot-tested (Appendixes A-D). Data collectors were trained and inter-rater reliability was determined. In February and March, visitors were tracked and their behavior recorded. From April through June, questionnaires were distributed at the hall's entrance and exit; interviews provided additional information concerning visitor understanding of the overall message and specific components; and interviews with museum security officers provided further information about visitor reactions. From July through August, data were tabulated and analyzed. In all, 13,552 visitors were studied from February through June. From August through December, the most feasible and cost-effective alterations were made, based on the evaluation.

Visitor Behaviors—Observations were made of 10,912 visitors ranging in age from under nine years to over 70 (Figure 1). Differences in gender representation were slight (Figure 2). Groups ranged in size from two to more than eight.

The study indicated that visitors used the exhibits well. No single unit was completely ignored, although very few covered the entire exhibit. The Biological Diversity exhibit had the greatest attraction; the Deforestation unit had the lowest. Of the 70 exhibit units, nine attracted more than 50 % of the visitors sampled. These included the four exhibits featuring scientists at work, At the River's Edge, and The Forest Doesn't Sleep at Night.

Some units attracted less than 10 % of visitors. Children aged nine years and under were less likely to stop and examine an exhibit unit than other age groups; nearly 90 % stopped at only 52 % of the exhibits and completely ignored 14 % of them-not surprising, since the targeted audience is the 7th grade and up. In contrast, 90 % of visitors aged 20 years and older stopped at nearly all (85 %) of the exhibits and completely ignored none.

The type and location of an exhibit affected attracting power. The most attractive were in direct sight lines; utilized diorama techniques; or included flips or oculars or objects unusual in size, color, or variety. The least attractive were those (1) opposite a highly attractive unit or (2) in an area where the path bifurcates, and (3) those having a great deal of text in relation to objects. For example, Harvesting the Sun contained 82 lines of text with four graphics that could be understood only by reading the text. In contrast, Biological Diversity had one 18-line label and hundreds of objects. The objects, rather than the label, were clearly the focus.

Time spent at individual exhibits is, of necessity, brief. Visitors spend an average of 22 minutes in the hall, and many want to see everything. The mean time at specific exhibits ranged from 4.1 seconds to 5 minutes, 34 seconds. Most visitors spent the most time at the five video theaters-the Rain Forest Theater in particular-and the least time at the Vanishing Forest mural.

Different age groups were attracted to different exhibit types. Manipulative exhibits (pushbuttons and flips) had high attractive power for all age groups. Those aged nine to 19 years were more attracted to exhibits containing oculars than other age groups. Those aged 60 years and older were more attracted to walkway units containing objects and labels than were other age groups. Generally speaking, the diorama-type exhibits of professional activities in biology and museums appealed to all age groups, particularly those under 60.

The hall includes 4 diorama-type exhibits:

- Scientist in the Canopy: a biologist in field gear surrounded by data-gathering equipment;
- The Scientist in the Field: a tropical biologist in a field station;
- The Scientist in the Museum: a research-station biologist at a desk studying specimens;
- Biotechnology: a molecular biologist at work using genetic research equipment.

The hall's five video theaters were most appealing to young children and teenagers. The Canopy Theater and the Rain Forest Theater had the highest attraction; the Cell Theater entrance video and the Research Theater had the lowest. All were used by over 50% of visitors and were consistently heavily occupied. The Rain Forest Theater held visitors for the longest period of time (Table 1). However, the behavior study showed that visitors in the theaters engaged in activities not related to the exhibition-resting, talking, eating, changing diapers, etc.

Distribution of Visitor Behavior—Visitor behavior varied with the type of exhibit. Overall, males and females exhibited all types of activity, and there were no major differences in their behavior. Although females exhibited more verbal interactions than males, the differences were not statistically significant ($p < .05$).

Meaningful interactive behaviors were exhibited by all age groups. Some merely looked at the colorful and unusual organisms; others read every label carefully. Still others scanned the labels to find specific information (Table 2).

All visitors most frequently exhibited visual behaviors. Otherwise, behaviors of visitors under 20 differed from those over 20. The younger group engaged in more non-exhibit-related behavior than older visitors and also tended to use manipulative exhibits to discover how flips worked and what buttons did rather than as learning resources. If results were pleasing, the action would be repeated. Older visitors were more likely to use manipulative devices meaningfully with intent to feel, see, or read.

Label reading occurred most often at manipulative exhibits. People read to learn what they needed to do. Exhibits featuring objects and explanatory labels also showed a high incidence of reading behavior. However, when visitors were asked during interviews, "What was the message of the exhibit you just saw?" Many responded, "I couldn't say. I was only looking at the beautiful plants and animals."

Verbal interaction was most often elicited by the diorama-type exhibits. The videos and manipulative exhibits also encouraged verbal group interaction.

Fatigue behaviors were most frequent at video theaters. This may not have been caused by the content-3% of visitors specifically reported having enjoyed them, and 20% looked at them-but because they were the only places in the hall that had ample seating and rest areas.

Questionnaires and Interviews—Analysis of study results indicated that the exhibits communicate different, yet accurate, messages. Results from 1,000 questionnaires suggest that the exhibition accomplished its basic mission, though the concept of commonality seemed less well understood than the other two-biodiversity and interrelationships. Many visitors left with new information about rain forests and an awareness of them as a beautiful and important resource in danger of being completely destroyed.

A large majority of visitors (96%) expressed a desire to return because they thought the exhibit interesting and enjoyable. They liked the design and feeling of being in a rain forest environment. Some felt that there was too much to see in one visit and that they may have missed some things. The amount of detail was stimulating and encouraged return visits. "There is so much to see; I will have to come back." Some intended returning to learn more. Others planned to report to family, friends, or school groups and return with them.

What Visitors Liked Best—In response to "What did you like best?" individual exhibits were mentioned most frequently (24%) (Table 3). Most-liked exhibits were those containing snakes, butterflies, spiders, monkeys, fish, and birds; dioramas showing scientists; the Tropical Waterfall, displaying macaws, parrots, and insects. Specifically mentioned were the flips, pushbuttons, trees, 3-D cases, special-effects lighting, sounds, models, rocks, the walkway, the mix of plants and animals, and the exhibit's colorfulness.

Also highly rated were informational presentations of deforestation, the danger rain forests are in, and comparisons with Wisconsin forests. The labels were described as "informative" and "easy to understand." Teachers made up a large percentage of visitors. They and others reported that the best things about the hall were its making learning easy, its being fun for all age groups, and its use of a variety of educational models.

Visitors also appreciated the accessibility to the handicapped, the evident and impressive amount of work invested in mounting the exhibit, and humor added to increase interest level.

What Visitors Liked Least—Of the visitors, 49% responded to "What did you like least?" Of these, 16% mentioned crowds; another 4% felt that the exhibit area was too small. The floor space between The Vanishing Rain Forest and Deforestation is approximately 5 feet. The addition of a simulated sloping rock and soil surface and barricade further reduced the space, which is used by visitors attending the exhibit and those who are simply passing by.

Negative reactions were mostly to content in specific exhibits-not their design. Creationists disliked the evolution exhibit. Visitors with an aversion to snakes, spiders, and bats did not like units containing them. Lack of reality was also a complaint. "Glass cases around the animals were distracting, carpeting didn't feel natural, there was no real plant life, it didn't rain, and the animals didn't move." Others felt the hall was too much like "Hollywood," because of so many videos.

Some wanted more labels that identified specific organisms; others felt there was too much to read.

The exhibit layout, which offered a variety of paths to follow (simulating actual forest conditions), confused some because it didn't lead from exhibit to exhibit without some backtracking; however, this layout may have contributed to the frequently expressed intent to return "to see everything." (The "explore-at-will" pathway was chosen by the design team because common-pathway biology exhibits in other museums were apparently unpopular). Other choices as "least liked" were the amount of walking needed, the repetitiveness in exhibits, the feeling of being visually overwhelmed, and being unable to find the handicapped access ramp.

GOAL 2: IMPROVING THE EXHIBITS

Recommendations based on the evaluation were made to increase visitor use and understanding of selected exhibits.

Increasing Attracting Power—Too few visitors stopped at seven units, but those who did spent a great deal of time. Moving a label or flip, changing a label or a label headline, or adjusting lights to increase attracting power were considered. In the cauliflory unit, which features rain-forest trees and shrubs that produce flowers and fruits directly from their trunks or main branches, improved lighting and sign placement was sufficient.

Increasing Holding Power—Visitors stopped at four exhibit units but did not spend much time. Instructions and identifications of objects were added to labels. For example, labels identifying the caiman and the anaconda and connecting the exhibit to the adjacent life-cycle exhibit were added to At the River's Edge. Explanatory and descriptive labels that answered overheard visitor questions were added to Biological Diversity. Brief labels were placed at points where visitors using the canopy walkway stopped to get a view of plant and animal life from above. Labels identified and silhouetted the ocelot and the jaguar and pointed out their common problems. The strangler fig tree exhibit shows a food chain; as a host tree rots away, a strangler fig tree flourishes inside it. New graphics and a new label, "The Strangler Strikes Again," were added to explain the process. The new signage was placed adjacent to the tree, and visitors, assuming that there was more to see and understand than a tree, spent more time at the exhibit.

The most easily implemented recommendations were carried out from August through December. New signage was installed in a total of eight exhibits; one was an identifying and descriptive label, "Slow Sloth," which had been perceived as a monkey. In 11 cases, signage was revised to clarify an exhibit's meaning. In still others, new components were added to tie together exhibits that visitors had not perceived as related. For example, an exhibit on natural selection united two components and encouraged visitors to use both to identify processes of natural selection.

GOAL 3: SETTING DIRECTIONS FOR FUTURE EXHIBITS

The summative evaluation provided useful directions for planning other exhibits. Some of the lessons learned may help other museums as well.

Summative Evaluations—The evaluation strengthened the team effort, a positive response that can be attributed to the project director and the designer, who had stated at the outset that evaluation would be made. However, while the evaluation identifies exhibits' high and low attractive and holding power, it does not explain why. It provides information, but the staff must interpret that information and make guesses on what to change to improve visitor reaction. In the case of the cauliflory exhibit, the staff discussed additional signage, sound, lighting, and more objects-and decided to try the least expensive, easiest suggestion first. Lighting and sign placement were changed and, in this instance, increased attractive power.

Summative evaluation also strengthened the staff's belief in the importance of getting visitors involved in design. A number of needed component changes became evident-more than could be coped with given the limited time, staff availability, and funding that we had.

Formative Evaluation—This should be a standard procedure in exhibit development for all major exhibitions as well as individual components. The study suggested that it should have been extended beyond the 14 prototypes that had been used in preparation of this exhibit. But formative evaluation has limitations. Exhibit mock-ups are shown out of context; sequences cannot be quickly, easily, or cost-effectively tested. However, it can measure how well and exhibit message is grasped.

The Team Approach—This, too, should be continued. The Rain Forest team was composed of curators, designers, educators, and a label writer. The curators determined the concepts for components and discussed them with the others, selected and prepared display objects, and checked exhibits for accuracy. The designer developed mock-ups for testing, in which all team members were involved. The educators worked with the label writer in coordinating the formative evaluation, coordinated the summative evaluation, and checked for exhibit understandability among visitors. It is crucial that participants place themselves at the service of the overall project. Back-and-forth input by team members must occur throughout the process.

Areas for Special Consideration—The evaluation pointed to areas needing special thought in the planning stages:

1. Video Theaters. The average length of time visitors spend in a hall should be considered in selecting presentations. The mean time visitors spent in the hall was 22 minutes out of an average of two hours for the entire Museum visit. The study also indicated that if many video theaters are to be used, formative evaluation should include focus visitor groups to evaluate their content.

Placement is also a consideration. The entrance may seem ideal for providing advance organization, but the Cell Theater is the least used of all the hall's theaters. On entering, visitors decide whether to go into a darkened room with a darkened screen or a large, lighted room full of plants, animals, pleasant sounds, and other people. The latter apparently has much greater attractive power.

2. Rest areas. Planning physically and visually restful spaces is important. The rain forest exhibit is visually exciting with an array of tropical trees, vines, leaves from many species varying in size and shape, tropical mammals, birds, insects and invertebrates, frogs and toads, and more. These high-intensity exhibit areas could be psychologically fatiguing, explaining why visitors stopped in areas with less visual stimulation.

3. Accommodation for groups. Since 90% of visitors come with at least one other person, design should provide for assembling groups, allowing adequate viewing for all, hearing the leader or guide, and interacting with each other and the exhibit.

4. The "you are there" approach. One of the most common responses of visitors asked what they liked best was the atmosphere, which made them feel as if they were actually in a rain forest environment. The Museum's style of creating a "you are there" atmosphere has come to be known as the "Milwaukee style" of exhibit design-one to which visitors react positively. Displaying objects in natural environments encourages verbal and nonverbal communication among visitors.

5. The "explore-at-will" layout. In contrast to a single pathway, one permitting visitors to choose their own pattern may contribute to their desire to return.

SUMMARY

On the basis of this extensive evaluation, we conclude that "Rain Forest: Exploring Life on Earth" is an effective exhibit in terms of getting its message across its first goal. It attracts visitors of all ages and holds their attention so they are encouraged to interact with the exhibit units. It presents a variety of exhibit styles, encouraging meaningful interaction and exhibit-related behaviors. It accomplishes its basic mission of communicating the educational themes of diversity, interrelationships, and commonality among living organisms as well as communicating the implicit exhibit messages, such as the importance and beauty of the rain forest and the need to preserve it.

ACKNOWLEDGEMENTS

We wish to thank the National Science Foundation Informal Science Education Program for generous support. We also thank data recorders Connie Brand, Meredith Platt, Carolyn Dehring, Mary Krebs, Edward Gesinski-Rose, Jeannine Santo, Susan Brahm, Coreen Dicus, Sally Groshek, Anna Chiger; tabulators Marian Witkowski, Joanne Korenic, Theresa Korenic, Edward Gesinski-Rose, and William Piper. Chandler Screven served as a resource person throughout the study; Meredith Platt, Connie Brand, Carol Ann Piggins, Eileen Korenic, Mary Buchaklian, and Jim Kelly served as editors of the original report. Diane Gawronski and William Hackbarth prepared the charts and graphs.

APPENDIX A: VISITOR TRACKING

Purpose. Provide information about public use of an exhibit and about exhibit appeal and measure which exhibits are approached, which avoided, and how much time visitors spend in the hall and at each exhibit.

Method. Data collector unobtrusively follows randomly selected visitors, recording their path and location and length of stops (Loomis, 1987: 220-225).

Sample. Individuals and groups (2 or more) over 7 years of age, except guided tour groups and students with worksheets.

Data recorders. Advanced undergraduate students from Marquette University and University of Wisconsin-Milwaukee, Museum exhibit designer and zoologist, all trained in using digital stopwatches, data recording sheets, and recording visitor movements.

Procedure.

1. Stand near entrance, wait for individual or group to enter. The first person to cross the threshold who fits the sample was tracked through the hall.
2. Record visitor's path without being noticed or influencing him/her. Indicate path with solid line on recording sheet. Complete additional data.
3. Mark visitor stops with an "X." Record time spent in exhibit-related behavior only.

Tabulation of data. Data were tabulated with a personal computer (Apple IIe) and Appleworks software.

APPENDIX B: RECORDING VISITOR BEHAVIOR

Purpose. Describe users of space and their activity.

Method. Data collectors record information about visitors at each exhibit station: location, gender, group size, activity (Hilke, 1988; Hayward, 1988). To record accurately, data collector must be close to but unobserved by visitor. Individuals arriving after observation began were not followed.

Sample. Individuals and groups (2 or more), except guided tours and students with worksheets.

Data recorders. Interns from Alverno College and Mount Mary College, a Museum zoologist, a Museum educator, a student aide, and an adult volunteer, all trained in recording behavior. Recording sheets were pilot-tested. Correlation among recorders was at least 80%.

Procedure. Data recording was done on four sheets, one for each observation selection in the hall. Sampling of behavior took place in seven 60-minute data-collecting sessions per day. Data recorded included number of visitors at each station, demographics of activity, and a brief objective description of behavior, at least one per individual. Visitors arriving after observation commenced were not recorded (resulting in a probable underestimation of behaviors). Once observations were completed-after visitors left or one minute passed-observer moved to next station. If no visitors were present, collector repeated the process. Observations were manually tabulated by Museum volunteers, a student aide, and a Museum educator, using procedures outlined by Diamond (1982).

APPENDIX C: ENTRANCE AND EXIT QUESTIONNAIRES

Purpose. To determine how and if the hall changed visitors' attitude and knowledge relating to biology in general and an understanding of diversity, interrelationships, and commonality of life organisms.

Method. Pre-testing determined incoming knowledge and attitudes and took place at the hall entrance. Post-testing determined exhibit effect and took place at the exit. One questionnaire was used. (Questions had been pilot-tested; some strategies were modeled after Borun [1977] and Screven [1976].) No visitor was tested at both locations. Participants were told that there were no right or wrong answers. Refusals to participate were recorded. Recorders were three Museum employees and a volunteer. Questionnaires were collected and the procedure repeated during the scheduled data-collecting period.

The 12-part questionnaire identified the respondent's age, sex, type of visit (individual or group), first-time or repeated visit, and sought to determine his/her knowledge of rain forests and temperate forests and interest in and information about biology as a career. In addition, a seven-section question tested grasp of exhibit content and message.

Sample. Individuals and groups over 12 years of age, except guided tour groups.

Tabulation of data. Data were tabulated manually by Museum volunteers.

APPENDIX D: VISITOR INTERVIEWS

Purpose. To determine the level of information visitors learn from targeted exhibits-those having especially high or low attraction and holding power-by interviewing non-cued visitors (whose interviews measure independent learning) and cued visitors (whose interviews measure learning under optimum conditions).

Sample. Individuals and groups over 12 years of age, except guided tour groups.

Data recorders. A Museum zoologist and a Museum exhibit designer trained in approaching and interviewing visitors and recording responses.

Method.

1. Fifty non-cued visitors were interviewed. Data collector standing near exhibit asked the first visitor fitting the sample who had already interacted with at east two exhibits if he/she would answer questions. Refusals were recorded. Consenting visitors' responses to three questions were recorded.

2. Fifty cued visitors were asked before they studied an exhibit if they would answer questions. Refusals were recorded. Consenting visitors were asked the same three questions, and their responses were recorded.

Mary Korenic is director of educational programming at the Milwaukee Public Museum where she conducts front-end analysis, formative, summative and remedial evaluation for both exhibits and public programs. She also serves as the 1999-2000 Chair of the Committee on Audience Research and Evaluation.

REFERENCES

Abrahamson, Dan; Gennaro, Eugene; and Heller, Patricia "Animal Exhibits: A Naturalistic Study." *Journal of Museum Education*: Roundtable Reports 8/2: 6-9, 1983.

Borun, Minda Measuring the Immeasurable: *A Pilot Study of Museum Effectiveness.* Philadelphia, PA: Franklin Institute Science Museum, 1977.

Diamond, Judy "Ethnology in Museums: Understanding the Learning Process." *Journal of Museum Education:* Roundtable Reports 7/4: 13-15, 1982.

Fronville, C. L., and Doering, Z. D. "Visitor Perspectives on Tropical Rainforests: A Report Based on the 1988 Tropical Rainforests: A Disappearing Treasure Information Study." Washington, DC: Smithsonian Institution, 1989.

Hayward, J. "Counting Visitors Helps to Evaluate Exhibits: A Case Study of Behavioral Mapping." *International Laboratory for Visitor Studies Review* 1/1: 76-85, 1988.

Hilke, D.; Hennings, E.; and Springuel, M. "The Impact of Interactive Computer Software on Visitors" Experiences: A Cast Study." *International Laboratory for Visitor Studies Review* 1/1: 34-49, 1988.

Korenic, M. "Literature of Museum Visitor Behavior as a Predictive Tool in Formative Evaluation of Museum Exhibits: An Illustration." Milwaukee Public Museum (in-house report), 1983.

Lee, R.S. "The Future of the Museum as a Learning Environment." In (Ed.) E. Bowles, *Computers and Their Potential Application in Museums.* New York, NY: Arno Press, 1968.

Loomis, R. Museum Visitor Evaluation: New Tool for Management. Nashville, TN: American Association for State and Local History, 1987.

Melton, A. Problems of Installation in Museums of Art. Washington, DC. AAM New Series, Number 14, 1935.

Olsen, M. "Staff and Visitor Relationships at the Milwaukee Public Museum," Dissertation, University of Wisconsin-Milwaukee, Milwaukee, WI, 1985.

Screven, C. "Exhibit Evaluation: A Goal-Referenced Approach." *Curator* 19/4: 271-290, 1976.

Shettel, H.; Butcher, M.; Cotton, T.; Northrop, J.; Slough, D. "Strategies for Determining Exhibit Effectiveness," Report No. AIR-E95-4/68-FR. Washington, DC: American Institutes for Research, 1968.

Young, A.M. "The Rain Forest in Milwaukee." *Curator* 32/3: 229-244, 1989.

CHAPTER 7

Issues in the Field

THE QUANDARIES OF AUDIENCE RESEARCH

Minda Borun and Randi Korn

Reprinted with permission of Museum Education Roundtable, "The Quandaries of Audience Research". *Journal of Museum Education* 20(1), 3-4, 1995. © Museum Education Roundtable 1995.

With federal agencies requiring evaluation plans as part of exhibit and program proposals and corporate and foundation funders increasingly interested in accountability, the audience research field is experiencing a growing demand for services. Suddenly, there is more work than the handful of trained professionals can handle. We are faced with a need to train additional practitioners, specify minimum standards of competency, define a museum staff evaluator position, and sharpen our focus on the central questions for this work.

STANDARDS OF PRACTICE

Since social science research involves talking to people, it might seem that anyone can conduct a study. Yes, anyone can talk to visitors and get a sense of what they think about an exhibit, program, or the museum as a whole, but the construction of a research study to uncover basic truths about the museum experience, or the development of an evaluation plan that gives actionable information about the effectiveness of museum presentations requires formal training in research techniques.

The Visitor Studies Association and the American Association of Museums' Committee on Audience Research and Evaluation (CARE) offer short, one- or two-day workshops to museum professionals. The intent of these workshops is to give participants a general overview of the evaluation process, to enhance their interest in conducting audience studies, and to enable them to work more effectively with research professionals. Unfortunately, these workshops have also produced a group of people who feel that they have become instant evaluators and the profession is now facing a serious problem of quality control. Some of the work that is being done does not meet acceptable standards of practice.

While we certainly do not want to limit access to the visitor studies field or to make its practices seem abstruse, it is important to point out that some basic training is required before you can conduct meaningful evaluation or research. Specifically, courses in experimental methods, interviewing techniques, and statistics are necessary in order to know how to set up a study, talk to visitors, and analyze and interpret data. This is not to say that a full graduate degree is required; on the other hand, it does take more than a one- or two-day workshop.

Good research design, sampling, validity, reliability, statistical testing, and content analysis procedures are critical concerns of research and evaluation. Experimental design of the plan for a study determines whether the data you collect will yield the information you seek. Proper sampling procedures ensure that the study group will represent the larger population you want to describe. A validity test looks to see if you are measuring what you think you are measuring. A reliability test tells you the likelihood that two independent observers will score the same event in the same way.

Statistical testing allows you to determine whether the relationships you observe are insignificant or likely to have occurred by chance. A judgment of "practical significance" considers whether the statistical difference is meaningful in the context of the questions being asked. The ability to judge practical significance comes only with experience. Finally, careful content analysis uncovers patterns in descriptive data obtained through open-ended interviews with visitors. All these procedures require training in research methods. If careful procedures are not used in the collection, analysis, and interpretation of data, you cannot have confidence in the results of a study or in any recommendations based on the results.

TRAINING

Closely related to the question of standards of practice is the issue of training future visitor studies professionals. If the visitor studies field is to grow and flourish, it needs a way to train new practitioners. In the past, the field has attracted primarily psychologists, with a few anthropologists and sociologists in the mix. These individuals have been through lengthy and expensive graduate training in social science research. One of the few alternatives to an advanced graduate degree in social science is to apprentice with one of the relatively small number of senior researchers in the field.

In 1986, Harris Shettel and Mary Ellen Munley conducted a survey of museum education and training programs and found that only five out of 56 graduate-level programs offered a course in evaluation techniques. Since their study, there has been some increase in the number of museum evaluation courses offered, but they are rarely required for a degree in museum studies or museum education. There is no degree program or even concentration in visitor studies for the would-be practitioner.

Clearly, we need to begin laying the groundwork for a program of graduate training in audience research that will allow students to acquire the necessary skills and experience to carry on and expand the visitor studies field.

IN-HOUSE EVALUATORS AND THE ORGANIZATION PLAN

Increasing numbers of museums are hiring in-house evaluators to assist with audience research and evaluation. These new staff members can fit into the museum's organizational structure in a variety of ways.

Ideally, evaluators should answer to a high-level, neutral staff member who is not aligned with any one department or project but who has the best interests of the museum in mind. If evaluations focus on products of the education or exhibits department, an evaluator should not report to the head of exhibits or education. The evaluator ought not to have a stake in the product being evaluated or be influenced, even unconsciously, by his or her supervisor's involvement with the product. Under no circumstances should the individual in charge of the project being evaluated be the individual responsible for writing the evaluator's performance review. It is best if the evaluator works in a neutral department-one removed from the planning and production of the product-and reports to a museum director, associate director, or vice-president.

ASKING THE RIGHT QUESTIONS

Museum researchers are continually challenged to design and implement studies demonstrating that people learn in museums. A few decades ago, when educational researchers were trying to measure cognitive outcomes in classrooms, museum researchers were doing the same with casual visitors in the museum exhibit environment. Measuring learning and understanding its complexities were stumbling blocks in both settings.

Over the years, our understanding of how people learn has evolved and broadened to include a wide range of abilities, skills, and intelligences. In response to this broader understanding and awareness, the ways in which we provide instruction, measure impact, and evaluate the museum experience must also evolve.

What is it that we want to know about visitor experiences? The experience researchers and evaluators have accumulated over the years contributes to and supports the methodological shift many of them have made from information to meaning, from measuring to understanding, and from results to process. This shift necessitates creative data collection methods and asks alternative questions. We are learning what not to ask visitors and are experimenting with new questions as we piece together the complexities of the visitor experience.

Concerns about asking the right questions are in part related to another methodological problem: most often, budget and time constraints demand that exhibit and program evaluation occur immediately after a visit, before visitors have time to process, internalize, or reflect on their experiences. Museum experiences, however, may not be fully realized during a museum visit, nor do they end when the visit ends. Even though evaluators continue to make important contributions to the visitor studies field, one must wonder what we may be missing by not being there to ask questions when visitors reflect on an experience they had in a museum a month ago, a year ago, or five years ago. Only recently have museum researchers begun to examine long-term effects of museum visiting.

Over the next decade, with enthusiasm and determination, researchers and evaluators will work together to meet the challenge of framing the questions that will move us closer to understanding the visitor experience and to measuring multiple outcomes.

RESEARCH AND PLANNING STRATEGY

Issues surrounding the audience research field will continue to evolve. This is true for any profession. Whatever the issues, they should not prevent any museum from including research in its planning strategy. Evaluation findings can be used to identify the qualities and shortcomings of particular programs and to determine whether learning and experience objectives are being met. If the museum community is concerned about its public image and the effect of its programs on visitors, these concerns should be reflected in a research and evaluation program.

NOTE

1. Harris Shettel and Mary Ellen Munley, "Do Museum Studies Programs Meet Evaluation Training Needs?" Museum News 64, no. 3 63-70. February, 1983.

AM
152
.I57
1999

C08508371

BORUN, Minda (ed.) et alii

INTRODUCTION TO MUSEUM

EVALUATION

BORROWER'S NAME	DATE RETURNED

Institute of Texan Cultures
Library

APPENDIX A

Bibliography

Sources of Articles in this Book in Order of Inclusion

Friedman, Alan. Convincing the Director. In *Museum Visitor Studies in the 90's.* Sandra Bicknell and Graham Farmelo (eds.), London: Science Museum 1993, 43-46.

Korn, Randi. Studying your Visitors: Where to Begin. In *History News*, 49 (2) March/April 1994, 23-26.

Hood, Marilyn G. Getting Started in Audience Research. In *Museum News*, Feb. 1986, 25-31.

Doering, Zahava. Manual for Interviewers. In *Role of the Interviewer in Survey Research*, January, 1999, 5-16.

Korn, Randi. Coding Data. In *Visitor Surveys: A User's Manual*, American Association of Museums, 1990, 50-55.

Ibid. Analyzing Data. Korn (1990), 69-78.

Ibid. Using Data. Korn (1990), 78-81

Borun, Minda *Front-End Evaluation: A Tool For Exhibit and Program Planning.* Unpublished Manuscript, 1993.

Rubenstein, Roslyn. The Uses of Focus Groups in Audience Research. In *Visitor Theory, Research and Practice. Proceedings of the 1990 Visitor Studies Conference 3*, Steven Bitgood (ed.) Jacksonville: Center for Social Design, 1990, 181-187.

Miles, Roger and Clark Giles. Setting Off On the Right Foot: Front-End Evaluation. In *Environment and Behavior*, 25 (6), Nov. 1993, 698-709.

Screven, Chandler. What is Formative Evaluation? In *Try It! Improving Exhibits Through Formative Evaluation.* Association of Science-Technology Centers, Washington, D.C., 1991, 8-13.

Griggs, Steven. Formative Evaluation of Exhibits at the British Museum (Natural History). In *Curator* 24 (3) Sept. 1981, 189-201.

Bitgood, Stephen and Shettel, Harris. The Classification of Exhibit Evaluation: A Rationale for Remedial Evaluation. In *Visitor Behavior,* Spring, 1994, 9 (1), 4-8.

Taylor, David. Team Practice in Remedial Evaluation Techniques With an Existing Exhibit. In *Try it! Improving Exhibits Through Formative Evaluation*, Association of Science-Technology Centers, Washington, D.C., 1991, 40-44.

Korenic, Mary S. The Rain Forest in Milwaukee: An Evaluation. In *Curator* 34 (2), 1991, 144-160.

Borun, Minda and Korn, Randi. The Quandaries of Audience Research. In *Journal of Museum Education* 20 (1), 1995, 3-4.

APPENDIX B

Resource Organizations

The AAM committee on Audience Research & Evaluation is a group of evaluators, curators, exhibit designers, educators, directors, managers, and others who believe that understanding visitors is an essential part of the planning and operation of museums and other public access cultural institutions. The committee plays an active role in the AAM and regional conferences by promoting papers, panel sessions, and workshops related to visitor studies.

AAM ANNUAL MEETING PROGRAMS

A good way to learn more about audience research and evaluation is by attending the AAM annual meeting. CARE sponsors sessions related to audience evaluation that are of interest to beginners, mid-level and advanced personnel in informal learning environments. These sessions illustrate how to do evaluation and how results are used for maximum impact.

In addition to sessions at the AAM annual meeting, preconference workshops which build skills in various evaluation techniques are frequently offered. Likewise, issues luncheons are very often offered during the AAM Annual Meeting allowing lively, interdisciplinary discussions over lunch. Poster sessions at the marketplace provide opportunity to meet with colleagues while learning about current evaluation research, methods, and results.

Best practices in the field are recognized through the Annual Exhibition Competition sponsored by the Curators Committee, National Association of Museum Exhibition (NAME) and CARE.

OTHER RESOURCES

Current Trends in Audience Research and Evaluation is a bound set of papers presented by CARE members at program and poster sessions. *Directory of Evaluators* is a listing of individuals and companies available to assist, consult, or conduct your evaluation projects.

BECOME A MEMBER OF CARE

Receive discounts on *Current Trends* and the *Directory of Evaluators.*

Receive *The Gauge*, a newsletter published twice a year that shares current information about audience research and evaluation.

Receive a membership directory of other members in CARE.

Be a part of a network of support for everyone interested in understanding museum audiences.

For more information about getting involved in CARE, contact the 1999-2000 Chair of Care, Mary Korenic, at 414-278-2716 or mary@mpm.edu or Milwaukee Public Museum, 800 W. Wells Street, Milwaukee, WI 53233.

AMERICAN EVALUATION ASSOCIATION

`http://www.eval.org/`

An international professional association of evaluators devoted to the application and exploration of program evaluation, personnel evaluation, technology, and many other forms of evaluation. Evaluation involves assessing the strengths and weaknesses of programs, policies, personnel, products, and organizations to improve their effectiveness.

VISITOR STUDIES ASSOCIATION

`http://museum.cl.msu.edu/VSA/`

More and more people throughout the world are spending more and more of their leisure time in environments that not only provide recreation, but have the potential to inform, enlighten, and educate. Such environments include museums, are galleries, visitor centers, aquariums, parks, zoos and other public-access recreational and educational facilities. The Visitor Studies Association (VSA) is a non-profit professional organization dedicated to the proposition that these facilities, in addition to meeting their own organizational objectives, should be effective in meeting the expectations, needs, and interests of the visitors.